METANOIA

METANOIA

Christian Penance and Confession

by STEPHAN RICHTER, O.F.M.

translated by Raymond T. Kelly

SHEED AND WARD : NEW YORK

Library of Congress Catalog Number: 66–22024

Cum permissu superiorum, February 11, 1964

Nihil Obstat
    Thomas J. Beary
    Censor Librorum
Imprimatur
    ✠ Robert F. Joyce
    Bishop of Burlington
    July 22, 1966

The Nihil Obstat and Imprimatur are official declarations that a book or pamphlet is considered to be free of doctrinal or moral error. No implication is contained therein that those who have granted the Nihil Obstat and Imprimatur agree with the contents, opinions or statements expressed.

Dedicated to both the Protestant and the
Catholic student communities in Kiel, in
affectionate memory of the years 1948–1958

Preface

Whatever Church community we adhere to, we Christians today are stirred more than any of our predecessors were by the words which our one Lord uttered on the eve of His Passion: *"that they should all be one!"* God's grace has taught us all to turn again to one another. And we seek to come together again not because our consciences are torn in the face of our modern world's profound alienation from God, but because what the Lord went on to say, "So let the world know that it is thou who hast sent me," has awakened our hearts and consciences to a responsibility shared indiscriminately by us all as Christians.

May this little volume render some small service in as many encounters between Christians as possible.

Dortmund, on the first day of the grand Week of Prayer for Unity among all Christians, January 18, 1964.

—FR. STEPHAN RICHTER, OFM

Contents

1

Metanoia

John the Baptist, the precursor of the Lord, initiated his preaching with precisely the same words that were to open the preaching of Him who was to follow and who was Himself the Word: "In those days John the Baptist appeared, preaching in the wilderness of Judaea; Repent, he said, the kingdom of heaven is at hand" (Matt. 3, 1f.).* And as we find in Mark 1, 15, our Lord began preaching the dawning of the kingdom of God with these words: "The appointed time has come, and the kingdom of God is near at hand; repent, and believe the gospel." The biblical expression for the reality to which both John and the Messiah Himself called humanity is *metanoia,* a term derived from the Greek verb *metanoein.* A brief look at any modern translation of the Bible will tell us that metanoia is given a wide variety of renderings, such as contrition, the performing of works of penance, conversion, changing one's heart, one's views, etc.

In the first place, it was not a new word coined by John or the Lord at all, but a term which was already rich in history. We shall limit ourselves here only to a brief review of the Old Testament period of expectation, without concerning ourselves with what *metanoia* might have meant in daily use when John and the Lord used it.

In the first chapter of the prophet Joel (which means, "the Lord is God"), we read:

> Citizens, hear and heed, ruler and commoner alike! . . . Weep bitterly, then, as maid that goes clad in sackcloth, untimely widowed. . . . Mourn, priests, and lament; in mourner's garb go about your work at the altar; ministers of God, to his presence betake you, and there, in sackcloth, keep vigil . . . for the Lord's help cry lustily. Woe betide us this day! The day of the Lord is coming; his the dominion, his the doom (Joel 1, 2–15, passim).

And then further on, it says:

> Time now, the Lord says, to turn the whole bent of your hearts back to me, with fasting and with mourner's tears. It is your hearts, not the garments you wear, that must be torn asunder. Come back to the Lord your God; he is ever gracious and merciful, ever patient and rich in pardon; threatens he calamity, even now he is ready to forgive (Joel 2, 12f.).

This text is important. For although conversion may be manifested in many outward forms, it is the *conversion of the heart* that is decisive. It is not the tearing of garments—which could easily be mere exhibitionism and theatrics before God and neighbor, and even before oneself—but the heart and its turning that is at issue here! To be sure, this conversion is possible only because God is "ever patient and rich in pardon," or as Jeremias expresses it,

> A time is coming, the Lord says, when I mean to ratify a new covenant with the people of Israel and with the people of Juda. It will not be like the covenant which I made with their fathers, on the day when I took them by the hand, to rescue them from Egypt; that they should break my covenant, and I, all the while, their master, the Lord says. No, this is the covenant I will grant the people of Israel, the Lord says, when that time comes. I will implant my law in their innermost thoughts, engrave it in their hearts; I will be their God, and they shall be my people. There will be no need for neighbor to teach neighbor, or brother to teach brother, the knowledge of the Lord; all will know me, from the highest to the lowest. I will pardon their wrongdoing; I will not remember their sins any more (Jeremias 31, 31–35).

At the beginning stands God, not man. Man always comes second in relation to God. The essence of sin consists precisely in man's wishing to come first, to be the beginning, middle, and end of things. The preaching of the prophets is always directed to making it clear to man that he must reserve the first place and center of his heart for God. The danger, indeed the greatest danger, for man lies precisely in attempting to appease his Creator and Lord with a few mechanical, outward works, while reserving the innermost part of his heart for other pieties. But the person who wishes to convert cannot do this.

What do I care, the Lord says, how you multiply those victims of yours? I have had enough and to spare. Burnt-offerings of rams, and the fat of stall-fed beasts, and the blood of calves and lambs and goats are nothing to me. Think you it is a welcome sound, the tramp of your feet in my courts bringing worship such as yours? Vain offerings, bring them no more. . . . Wash yourselves clean, spare me the sight of your busy wickedness, of your wrongdoing take farewell. Learn, rather, how to do good, setting your hearts on justice, righting the wrong. . . . Crimson-dyed be your guilt, it shall turn snow-white; like wool new-washed yonder scarlet stain. [All this was the preparation for the words that come next.] Will you think better of it, and listen, and have rich harvests to feed you? (Isaias 1, 11–13, 16–19).

At stake then is the new spirit, the conversion of the heart, indeed nothing less than a new heart. "Cor mundum crea mihi, Deus—My God, bring a clean heart to birth within me," is the prayer of David, bent under heavy guilt, in the fiftieth Psalm. It is not a question here of this or that deed, but of turning, in one's innermost heart, truly to God. Everything depends upon this turning-point, for "They shall be my people, and I their God, once in good earnest they have retraced their steps, and come back to me" (Jeremias 24, 7).

Thus John's preaching of penance and conversion did not constitute an absolute departure at all. On the contrary, the basic tenor of this prophetic utterance was thoroughly familiar to the pious ears of Israel. To be sure, the Israelites were all too accustomed to relating such warnings and calls to con-

version spoken in God's name to thieves, adulterers, prosti-
tutes, tax collectors, etc., rather than to themselves. But
John's call to a change of heart was meant not only for heathens
and confirmed sinners. Indeed, it pointed with special vehe-
mence to the so-called holy individuals, to those who regarded
themselves as soundly religious and good. It is significant that
the precursor of the Lord begins his preaching with the words
of Isaias, so familiar to the Jews: "There is a voice of one
crying in the wilderness, Prepare the way of the Lord,
straighten out his paths. Every valley is to be bridged, and
every mountain and hill levelled, and the windings are to be
cut straight, and the rough paths made into smooth roads, and
all mankind is to see the saving power of God" (Isaias 40, 3–
5; Luke 3, 4–6).

For to the multitudes that came out to be baptized he spoke
in these terms: "Who was it that taught you, brood of vipers,
to flee from the vengeance that draws near? Come then, yield
the acceptable fruit of repentance; do not think to say, We
have Abraham for our father; I tell you God has power to
raise up children to Abraham out of these very stones. Already
the axe has been put to the root of the trees . . ." (Luke 3,
7–9, but cf. the entire chapter). How can we explain such
hard words coming from John?

What is it that moves the evangelists to open their call to
penance with this unrestrained sharpness and then, in much
more moderate tones, to plead with those hated professional
exploiters, the soldiers and publicans, for a change of heart?
Without doubt the synoptic authors have given us here an
almost pure piece of original doctrinal substance. For the
person and words of John stood far too clearly in view to

be subjected to any kind of misrepresentation. But as he preached penance and conversion, his eyes fell especially upon the professionally pious Pharisees, "who had confidence in themselves, thinking they had won acceptance with God, and despised the rest of the world" (cf. Luke 18, 9ff.).

No longer were the works of man to be finally decisive in religion. No longer was the basic question to be that of how often a man fasted in a week, or how many prayers he recited, or how many alms he gave. For all such things could be performed with a view to self-justification or self-redemption, needing God only as an endorsement or as mere decoration. Or what is worse, such works might be aimed at rendering God indebted to man. The relationship Creator-creature would thus be turned upside-down—and the worst of it is that when this happens, one does not even realize it. The frightening reference to serpents and broods of vipers truly belongs here in all its force and stringency.

The *chassidim* or Pharisees were a lay group of merchants, officials, and other men of the people who were banded loosely together and who strove, under the leadership of the scriptural scholars, to live an exemplary life according to the law (including all its additions of human origin). Their rule of conduct, however, was the sinfulness of their neighbor: "I am not like him!" The Pharisee fixed his sights on other men rather than upon Him who alone is holy and who, even from the time of Moses, calls: "You must be set apart, the servants of a God who is set apart" (Lev. 11, 44). True conversion takes for its measure the holiness of God, in the face of which every man must call out with Isaias: "Alas, said I, that I am lost; my lips, and the lips of all my countrymen,

are polluted with sin . . ." (Isaias 6, 5). And it was to this
holiness of the inner man that John wished to convert men.
As a sign of this change of heart his penitents received baptism
with water. Outward signs were always used to symbolize
what transpired in the innermost soul of man: "Wash me
clean, cleaner yet, from my guilt" (Psalm 50, 4). God alone
could wash clean; the works of man should then follow as
"fruits of penance" which came especially in the form of
effective love for one's neighbor: "The man who has two
coats must share with the man who has none; and the man
who has food to eat, must do the like" (Luke 3, 11). It is not
a question of works whereby one might establish justification
before God or even a question of the assurances so esteemed
by the Pharisees, but always and exclusively that of the great
human attitude in dealing with God: "God, be mercifull to
me; I am a sinner."

Before considering what conversion, penance and change of
heart mean in the speech of "the only-begotten of the Father,
out of whose fullness we have all received grace upon grace,"
we must first of all consider the fact that this is one of the
most fundamental thoughts of the whole New Testament. At
the very beginning of discipleship stands the profession—not
with lips alone, but with the heart—of absolute poverty, the
act of delivering oneself totally to Him who is the Way, the
Truth, and the Life of men (cf. Matt. 5, especially the
beatitudes). When there is not hunger, but contentment;
when self-justification or self-satisfaction prevails with its
scornful view of others rather than realistic sadness over one's
own state of perdition, when hardness against oneself is
avoided but is recommended for others, then we can say that

the basic premisses for a breakthrough into the kingdom of God are lacking. In his following of the Lord, the disciple always lives by this basic position of the beatitudes, precisely because he knows himself to be always at the point of a breakthrough. He can never say: "I have come far enough here in my living and striving for conversion and perfection," for he can never forget the words: "When you have done all that was commanded you, you are to say, We are servants, and worthless" (Luke 17, 10). Is this what really marks the intense striving for perfection which the saints, for example, have practiced in their daily lives? Is the Lord possibly understating it here? And is not the disciple, who is honestly making the effort day in and day out to follow Him, perhaps also understating it? Can sincerity really keep pace with the following of Christ? Indeed, is sincerity enough? It depends upon the measure, upon the effectiveness, of the resultant perfection!

And we read at one point: "But you are to be perfect as your heavenly Father is perfect" (Matt. 5, 48). This was preceded indeed by the great comparison, "Do not the heathen also do this?" (One should reread carefully the entire chapter of the Sermon on the Mount, for it is essential as a foundation for what we shall say concerning *metanoia* in the main part of our study!) But in his conversion, the disciple sets out on the way every day afresh, orienting himself anew to the perfection of the Master, for "God has kindled a light in our hearts, whose shining is to make known his glory as he has revealed it in the features of Jesus Christ" (II Cor. 4, 6) and, as the Lord Himself told Philip, "Whoever has seen me, has seen the Father" (John 14, 9). Indeed, the disciple prays daily that God the Father's will may be done on earth as it is done in heaven. How lightly do these requests (and others of the Lord's Prayer) pass over our lips? Martin Luther's words on this point, where he claimed that the greatest of all martyrs was the Lord's Prayer, are unfortunately all too true even today. Reinhold Schneider, in his very rich study of the Lord's Prayer, says of this request concerning the Father's will:

> What existence could dare to compare itself, even in the smallest degree, to that absolute order? And even if the unspeakably difficult should come to pass, even if our will should become one with that of the Father, would not then those inclinations and desires, those dreams over which we hold no sway, still contradict His will? . . . How could it ever be? How could there ever be an obedience on earth which would be like that Being in obedience? But it is not ours to ask this. Rather should we pray that it be in fact so, and we should accept the will of God. The beginning of glory is accomplished, for God's Son is among us. . . . The works that proceed from union with the Son, here is the will of the Father. . . .[1]

We men shall always be beginners on this way, precisely because we remain, in spite of God's call to follow His Son, in spite even of all grace, creatures capable of real sin. Until the day of harvest, our heart will remain like the field in which the sower sowed only good seed, but which overnight showed an overwhelming quantity of weeds (cf. Matt. 13, 24ff.). Weeds among wheat, or perhaps more exactly, wheat among weeds, this is our situation. But our yardstick of perfection remains that of the Father who became visible to us in His Son! Consequently it is a question of thinking anew, in the light of our daily state of loss, about ourselves and all things. It is a matter of reconsidering our cult of self and our subjection to inferior drives. For we are no longer bound to a law as our final norm. We are bound instead to Him who personally revealed Himself to us as "the good shepherd of our souls" (I Peter 2, 25).

The Apostles repeatedly spoke of the "new birth" and of the "new man who is made according to God in justice and true holiness," constantly intoning the hymn of praise of the redeemed: "See how the Father has shown his love towards us; that we should be counted as God's sons, should be his sons" (I John 3, 1). And in this, they understood their Master well. But in the same connection it is precisely the beloved disciple of our Lord who sets up the requirement: "A man who rests these hopes in him lives a life of holiness; he too is holy" (I John 3, 3).

It is at this point that the apostolic Church's expectation of the end of the world comes dramatically into play. The coming of the Lord struck the "eleventh hour," calling us to take advantage of His presence. Now it is a question of running the "holy race" and of striving for the garland of victory. One must take care not to miss the *kairos,* the moment which is the raison d'être of it all. And this is always the same, namely, "the today of God."[2] It is this "today" that one must acknowledge and live daily, that to which one must never close or harden his heart (Psalm 94) as the chosen people did in the desert. For God, it is always today, and consequently, "since you hear His voice, harden not your hearts." It is a question of starting out afresh every day: "The man who tries to save his life will lose it; it is the man who loses it that will keep it safe" (Luke 17, 33). The grain of wheat must fall ever deeper into the earth, so that it can bring forth fruit with the Lord. Daily we must rise up again from sleep, for salvation draws nearer with each day (cf. the teaching with which every new Church year opens in the lesson of the Mass for the First Sunday of Advent).

Paul himself is an example of the faithful following of the beloved Master, and this becomes more and more his only passion: "Him I would learn to know, and the virtue of his resurrection" (Phil. 3, 10). It was a Christocentric longing that drove Paul onward: "Not that I have already won the prize, . . . I only press on . . ." (Phil. 3, 12).

What the prophets preached as a change of thinking and John took up as the fundamental attitude for preparing the way for the Lord, and what the Master Himself invoked as the foundation for discipleship, is one and the same: *Change your heart, change your thinking, welcome the kingdom of God as a child.* This is what Peter, Paul, John, and all the great saints of the Church have lived and re-lived at all times.

The following-in-the-footsteps-of-the-Lord preached by the first Pope is found again as the all-embracing ideal of such a saint as Francis of Assisi. Thus we find him quoted, in Thomas of Celano's life of St. Francis,[3] as saying: "Brothers, let us now begin at length to serve the Lord God, for up to now we have made little if any progress." (And this, incidentally, was shortly before his death!) And on another occasion, Francis says: "Had the Almighty poured such graces upon a thief, he would have been more grateful than you, Francis." With profound insight, Celano comments here: "Thus was Francis wont to speak to himself, when others praised him."

Notes

* The Biblical quotations used in this book are taken from *The Holy Bible*, trans. Ronald Knox. Copyright © 1944, 1948 and 1950 by Sheed & Ward, Inc., New York. With the kind permission of His Eminence the Cardinal Archbishop of Westminster.

1. Reinhold Schneider, *Das Vaterunser*, 3rd ed. (Freiburg im Breisgau, 1962), pp. 42ff.

2. Roger Schutz, *Das Heute Gottes* (Freiburg im Breisgau, 1963). Cf. also Roger Schutz, *Living Today for God* (New York, Taplinger).

3. Thomas von Celano, *Leben und Wunder des hl. Franziskus von Assisi*, translation, introduction, and notes by Engelbert Grau, OFM, Fransiskanische Quellenschriften, 5 (Werl. in W., 1955), pp. 181, 361.

2

Justification
and the Penitential Act
Required of the Christian

It is not the purpose of this volume, nor would it be possible within its narrow limits, to set forth even the fundamental positions of the Christian doctrine of justification. Nevertheless, the relationship between justification and sin, or better, the impossibility of beginning a new life without contrition, must necessarily be reviewed.[1]

Many people have been divided on this question (not only this question, to be sure, but it was one of the basic ones!). We must succeed in seeing the whole matter in context and try to understand one another again. Perhaps our hope lies in Vatican II, which has defined itself more clearly and humanly on the question of justification than the sharply exclusive Catholic answer to this question formulated by the Council of Trent.

Heinrich Ott put us all on a new track when he wrote: "Luther's formula, "Simul peccator—simul justus (at once both sinner and justified) also fits into this tension between

the visible and the invisible realities of faith. Man, even the
believer, is visibly a sinner who has to struggle daily with his
sins. (This refers us to the experience of sin or sinfulness.
We must come back to believing that sin is "sin," that it is
an offense against *God*, and that man is a sinner.) But it is
an invisible reality of faith that, precisely as believer, man is
justified before the tribunal of God. He can neither see nor
experience this justification. Yet faith is faith precisely in that
it rests upon the *promissio,* the promise of what he neither
sees nor experiences" (Hebrews 11, 1).[2] We all know that the
Council of Trent (Denz. 799, 821) rejected this phrase of
Luther, because it was presented as a metaphysical proposition. But is it so clear that Luther intended a metaphysical
proposition in those words?

In any case contemporary Protestant theology interprets
this statement of Luther in many different ways. Does Hans
Küng interpret Karl Barth correctly? Does Barth interpret
Luther correctly? Are we making progress here at all? Can
we as Catholics not take a positive attitude, one that has value
for the simple position of the lay Christian, toward this fundamental axiom of the Reformation? Or are we perhaps more
confused and more separated than even our fathers were?

THE MESSAGE OF THE GOSPEL

All the differences between us notwithstanding, and apart
from every form of theological controversy, we can all assent
to the following words in the First Epistle of St. John: "See
how the Father has shown his love towards us; that we should

be counted as God's sons, should be his sons. . . . If a man is born of God, he does not live sinfully, he is true to his parentage. . . . This then is how God's children and the devil's children are known apart. A man cannot trace his origin from God if he does not live right, if he does not love his brethren" (I John 3, 1, 9f.). The same St. John, who does not tire of calling for a "birth from God" (cf. John 3; the conversation with Nicodemus, etc.), says with perfect naturalness from the very beginning in the same First Epistle:

What, then, is this message we have heard from him, and are passing on to you? That God is light, and no darkness can find any place in him; if we claim fellowship with him, when all the while we live and move in darkness, it is a lie; our whole life is an untruth. God dwells in light; if we too live and move in light, there is fellowship between us, and the blood of his Son Jesus Christ washes us clean from all sin. Sin is with us; if we deny that, we are cheating ourselves; it means that truth does not dwell in us. No, it is when we confess our sins that he forgives us our sins, ever true to his word, ever dealing right with us, and all our wrongdoing is purged away. If we deny that we have sinned, it means that we are treating him as a liar; it means that his word does not dwell in our hearts (I John 1, 5–10).

Let these Johannine words suffice without adding various Pauline texts which would also be appropriate here, and let us attempt to discover the theme that holds them together.

And I ask the reader to bear in mind all the texts of the New
Testament that deal with being children of God, new life,
new creation, birth from God, and rebirth on the one hand,
and on the other hand those that make reference to the
dangers abroad for the redeemed man, his inclination to sin
and to falling back into his old servitude of sin, those that
exhort him to watchfulness and care, and those that deal with
contrition, conversion, change of heart, etc.

It stands as indubitably clear in the message of good news
of the New Testament that by virtue of the redeeming death
of our Lord on the Cross and by virtue of our being included
in Christ's death and resurrection, we are de facto redeemed
and we in fact share in the "mystery of the redeemed."[3] We
are "washed clean," "buried and risen again with him," a gift
which comes with the spirit of being a child, unmerited and
unmeritable. Paul leaves no room for doubt here (cf. Romans
6). It is not as if something were merely covered over, as if
God, like a grand lord, simply looked the other way regarding
the facts which in reality, however, continued to stand. No,
God never closes His eyes, if we may put it anthropomor-
phically. Whatever He does, He does absolutely. We have
been cleansed from original sin on the one hand, and we
have been given, on the other hand, a new life by virtue of
being born of God. This is the basic tenor of the whole salvation message in general. Does God only *speak* justly? Or does
He also *act* justly? Does God only cover things over, or does
He change what was unholy into what is holy, what was un-
justified into what is justified, those who were servants into
free men, those who were strangers into members of his

family, those who were slaves into inheritors, into co-inheritors with Christ? Read John 3 and Romans 6 and the entire First Epistle of St. John!

THE DOCTRINE OF JUSTIFICATION OF THE COUNCIL OF TRENT

The Church stated her belief, in the Council of Trent, in these terms:

For the Apostle's words, "It was through one man that guilt came into the world; and, since death came owing to guilt, death was handed on to all mankind by one man. In him all had sinned" (Rom. 5, 12), must be understood in the same sense that the Catholic Church, universal in the whole world, has always understood them. Precisely because of this rule of faith, even children, who have not yet been able to commit sins of any kind, are baptized according to apostolic tradition, in order truly to forgive their sins, so that in them, through rebirth, that which was imputed to them through their very conception, is made clean. For "whosoever is not reborn by water and the Holy Spirit cannot enter into the kingdom of God" (John 3, 5). . . . For God hates nothing in those who have been reborn, because there is nothing worthy of condemnation in those who are "really buried with Christ in death through baptism" (Romans 6, 4), those who "do not follow the ways of flesh and blood" (Romans 8, 1), but who "are quit of the old self, and the habits that went with it, and are

clothed in the new self, that is being refitted all the time
for closer knowledge, so that the image of the God who
created it is its pattern" (Eph. 4, 22–34; Col. 3, 9–10),
who have become flawless, unspotted, pure, guiltless and
thus beloved sons of God, heirs of God, sharing the inheritance of Christ (Romans 8, 17), so that nothing
holds them back any longer from entrance into heaven.
But the holy council of the Church knows and acknowl-
edges that concupiscence, or the source of its fire, remains
in the baptized. Since, however, it was left there in order
that they may struggle for the victory, it cannot harm those
who do not consent to it but bravely resist it through the
grace of Christ Jesus. On the contrary, "the first share in
the harvest goes to the laborer who has toiled for it" (II
Tim. 2, 5).[4]

It is so liberating to find, precisely in this Magna Charta
of the Catholic doctrine of justification, the holy revealed
word of God quoted directly time and again. Does the Catholic position not draw *directly* from God's word? As a matter
of plain fact, it supports Luther's *simul justus et peccator* in
its proper sense. Is it possible that the reformer understood
this expression *only* in the sense of concrete salvation history
—being misunderstood as having meant it metaphysically—
and that only in our generation has an understanding finally
become possible again?

Otherwise, where is the dividing line? Perhaps in the question as to what an adult should do, or rather cannot do, when
he is preparing as an unbaptized person for the sacrament of
rebirth? What has to happen in order that a baptized person

who has turned from God in serious sin might find God's mercy again? The classical teaching precisely for this second case was given to us by the Lord Himself in the parable of the prodigal son (Luke 15).

It seems to me that this parable presents us with something decisive for justification in general, and that any genuine considerations of this important matter must turn at some point to a careful study of this parable. In the beginning we *always* find God's mercy, we *always* find His fatherly heart yearning for all His children, but especially for the one who went astray. The older "faithful son" (but how faithful is he really?) seems not to give the father any concern. It is the younger son who stubbornly demands his part of the inheritance: "Father, give me that portion of the estate which falls to me." He then goes to a faraway country and squanders his share of his father's estate. It seems that it went mainly to gambling and women. The father waits and waits. The son is free. He is not a slave, but a son who should become an inheritor of his father's house. But as soon as the son approaches even in the distance, the father rushes to meet him, embraces him, and orders the celebration of a feast . . . whereupon the faithful older son is scandalized and calls his father to an accounting of all that he, the faithful son, did while remaining at home, and reminds him of the share of the inheritance which he had not demanded, even though he might have. And he points out that the father never gave him anything like such a welcome, etc. Where indeed lies the real prodigality?

Everything seems to be contained in these few sentences. God is *always* waiting with mercy and forgiveness for *every-*

one, but He does not hang on a person, He does not push Himself on anyone. Since a son is a son, and the creature is the likeness of its maker, the son must want and be prepared to accept the mercy of his Father. Here we have in its purest form the Pauline phrase, "by grace alone," or the words of the Apostle to his beloved Ephesians: "Yes, it was grace that saved you, with faith for its instrument; it did not come from yourselves, it was God's gift" (Eph. 2, 8). And yet the same Apostle must warn them (II Cor. 6, 1f.)—and so does the Church warn her children at the beginning of every Lenten season—"And now, to further that work, we entreat you not to offer God's grace an ineffectual welcome. I have answered thy prayer, he says, in a time of pardon, I have brought thee help in a day of salvation. And here is the time of pardon; the day of salvation has come already."

Man must admit that he is a sinner, he must acknowledge and make room for God's mercy. Indeed the entire matter depends upon a definite admission of guilt and not upon a vague recognition of the possibility of fault. It is quite clear that the Church's teachings (cf. Denz. 799, 801, 822, 1793) mean precisely this and nothing else. That this faith finds outward expression, that this conversion takes the form of definite action (as in the parable, the prodigal son rises up and goes to his father) is as self-evident as the fact that love does not remain speechless and motionless, but moves toward externalization, communication, and demonstration.

It would seem that the words of St. Augustine of Hippo, spoken before any division came into the Church, come simply and clearly to the point here: "God, who created thee without thyself, will not redeem thee without thyself."

GOD'S MERCY AND HUMAN MERIT

The question of merit, to a great extent as a result of the corrupt custom of calculating, weighing, counting, etc., especially in the practice of indulgences of the sixteenth century, seems to have evoked an indescribable repugnance in Luther. (Sartre presents us, in his drama *Le Diable et le bon Dieu*, with the most extreme subtleties in these matters precisely in the indulgence sequence. It may well have been thus. What a frightening confusion!)

But *must* the question of merit still be an insurmountable wall for us *today?* Is there not in the holy Gospel a way of speaking about merit which deals with the reality in an uncomplicated way and which is acceptable to *every person* of good will?

It would appear that our Lord's image of the good tree which brings forth good fruit and the bad tree which yields bad fruit (cf. Matt. 7, 17 ff.) could, in its simplicity and straightforwardness, resolve much of our difficulty. It is of the essence of Christian life that because of his bond with Christ (cf. the parable of the vine and the branches, John 15, 1 ff.), the baptized person shares by grace—provided, of course, that he has not severed himself from Christ by sin— in the very life of Christ, and thus also in the fruit of that life, especially the fruit of love. One is forced here to see the relationship of the person living in a communion of love with his Lord just as organically as our Lord sees it in the image of the vine and the branches or as Paul sees it in his image of the one body with its many members (1 Cor. 12, 12 ff.). And we find here the word "reward," which falls so hard upon

Protestant ears, clearly pronounced by the lips of the Lord Himself: "Be glad and light-hearted, for a rich reward awaits you in heaven" (Matt. 5, 12). Or in another text: "And every man that has forsaken home, or brothers, or sisters, or father, or mother, or wife, or children, or lands for my name's sake, shall receive his reward a hundredfold, and obtain everlasting life" (Matt. 19, 29). Moreover, the Gospel distinguishes sharply between the lazy and the faithful servants, and between the wise and the foolish virgins.

It will not be easy to deny that the Lord Himself gave expression to the idea of reward and merit. And He takes no middle position in this. The image of the tree and its fruit is utterly explicit, as is that of the vine and its branches or that of the body and its members. At no point, however, do we encounter anything that smacks of a principle of ability or achievement such as "God, behold here my accomplishments and merits for which You owe me this and that—and naturally eternal life!" Indeed our Lord warns with unmistakable clearness against this attitude, condemning it as extreme pharisaism. But who would deny that Christians are also capable of it, as dangerous as it is?

In the parable of the laborers in the vineyard (Matt. 20, 1–16), which the Church presents to us year after year in preparing us for Lent on Septuagesima Sunday, our Lord draws a divinely sovereign line through all of our human thinking about wages, reward, and every form of calculation. Indeed it is fundamental for the Christian life to look more frequently and more deeply into the substance of this parable.

And is it not also possible that the theological speculation concerning *meritum de congruo* and *de condigno* fits finally into its proper perspective here? Since these considerations have no particular significance for the daily life of the Christian in the imitation of his beloved Master, however, we will not concern ourselves with them further than this remark. Coming back to the highly important parable of the laborers in the vineyard, it is of the utmost importance to practice daily the lesson that we are all without exception dependent on the goodness and mercy of God, so that we may wish in our innermost hearts the mercy of God for every man without exception. "Or are you envious that God is good?" Or do you not believe that God can do as He pleases?

We touch here on the very foundation of the spiritual life of the Christian.[5]

THE MESSAGE OF LUTHER

Recently I had the opportunity to stand before the doors of the Church in Wittenberg where, on the eve of All Saints 1517, the Augustinian monk Martin Luther nailed his ninety-five theses.[6] Today, they can be read by all in large letters on a plaque in the back of the church.

Following are some of the words the reformer used on that occasion—and what a catastrophe these words were to call forth in the Christian body!

1. Our Lord and Savior Jesus Christ meant, with the words "Do penance!" etc., that the entire life of the believer must be a penance.

2. Hence His Word may not be understood as the penance of the sacrament of penance (i.e., as the confession and execu-

tion of special acts of penance which are solemnly administered through the priestly office).

3. However, it does not mean only an interior penance having no outward expression in self-mortification.

4. Therefore, as long as hatred toward oneself (which is the true interior penance) remains, and it must remain until the kingdom of heaven comes, punishment for sin will stand (which is the outward penance, or self-mortification).[7]

There is no question about the fact that an interior necessity drove the reformer to this step which then released an avalanche which no one was able to control. Even if the question of indulgences assumes a central role in the following theses, the reality of his real concern remains open and clear: Luther was concerned with genuine penance! And he saw genuine penance menaced, even undermined, by the indulgence practices of his day. Even the all too formal administration of the sacrament of penance caused him great inner anxiety and concern. To be sure, there are many false propositions in these theses of Luther, but all of this could have turned to the good were a better theology of the sacrament of penance available to him at the time.

Certainly, we cannot concur in the absolute distinction and separation of penance and confession proposed even in the first two theses. Indeed, their relationship to one another will be taken up in detail in the next chapter.

Let us hold fast to the following points—and it would be highly desirable for Protestant and Catholic Christians alike to hold these things in common, indeed to learn from one another in these matters:

1. The Protestant "simul justus et peccator" should be understood to mean, if we take as our foundation the Johannine and Pauline statements on the question, that, although we are "truly beloved of God" and adopted sons through His generous graces, we nevertheless are and remain true sinners. We understand this in that simple clarity which comes through in John's words: "Sin is with us; if we deny that, we are cheating ourselves; it means that truth does not dwell in us" (I John 1, 8).

2. In no way, however, may any understanding of that fundamental Protestant proposition (even though this understanding comes from a total view of revelation and from genuine theological reflection) call into question either the fact that justification *really occurs* with baptism, or the reality of "a new creation," "birth from God," "rebirth," or the fact that the baptized person has been given by grace a new form of existence which Paul saw fit to call "being in Christ Jesus."

3. This work of the new creation is the work of God's unmerited and unmeritable love.

4. This does not exclude, but rather implies, that the human person opens himself to God. For man can also close himself to God. God never infringes upon man's arbitrary use of freedom in any way at all, and neither does He ever take away His constant offer of grace. With God it is always today: "Today, if you hear His voice, harden not your hearts."

5. Since he is on a pilgrimage, even the man of grace and justification is always in danger: "We bear the treasure of our calling in earthen vessels," says Paul.

6. Penance, change of heart, conversion is the *life*-task of the Christian and must be practiced anew every day.

7. This penance is not merely interior, no matter how important a role the "contrite and humble heart" (Psalm 50) plays, but it also exteriorizes itself, especially in works of love, in the fulfillment of the *mandatum magnum* (the "great commandment"). How clearly this concerned Luther in the theses 43, 44, 45, and 46, for example, even though—which was very understandable—it was always bound up with his objection to the misuse of indulgences! "Let Christians be taught that he who gives to a poor or needy person does better than if he had bought indulgences for himself. For it is through the works of love that love grows and man becomes better. . . ."

8. The disciple of the Lord always observes the Master's admonitions to wakefulness and prayer, and is ever mindful of His warning, "lest you fall into temptation." But at the same time, he hopes to obtain God's grace, knowing that God "will not play you false; that he will not allow you to be tempted beyond your powers" (I Cor. 10, 13).

9. Since the baptized person stands in a living bond with his Lord—"I am the vine, you are the branches," "And you are Christ's body, organs of it depending upon each other"— he shares in the life of Christ and also, by virtue of this bond of grace, in the fruits of the work of Redemption—performed once for all time. He also knows that he is called to "bring forth fruit with patience," and indeed that God's gracious mercy accepts as genuine merit even one's ineffectual efforts in the imitation of Christ. This calling makes the true disciple of Christ all the more humble and merciful. He is never proud, never self-complacent, never self-justified. For he recog-

nizes with St. Augustine that all of our achievements are only gifts of God.

10. With the teaching of his Church, the disciple knows that he can never reach an absolute certainty of salvation before his definitive reception in the heavenly presence of the Lord, which means never before death and judgment. He knows that he and all men are totally and absolutely dependent upon the "gentle and easy mercy" of God (Bernanos).

11. Neither does the Christian understand penance negatively, but sees himself rather positively before his goal of "becoming perfect, as his Father in heaven is perfect."

12. In his imitation of Christ, the baptized person strives daily to come nearer to this goal, placing complete trust in the grace of the Lord and making a constant effort to "grow into the maturity of Christ" in collaboration with the help which constantly precedes, supports, and accompanies him on his way.

Penance, conversion, renewal, and change of heart and mind thus become a total effort of the Christian's life, pervading the entirety of his existence. But the Christian is always mindful of the words of the Lord: "When you have done all that was commanded you, you are to say, We are servants, and worthless" (Luke 17, 10).

Notes

1. Hans Küng, *Justification: The Doctrine of Karl Barth and a Catholic Reflection* (New York, Nelson, 1965). See also Hans Urs von Balthasar, *Karl Barth. Darstellung und Deutung seiner Theologie* (Cologne, 1951).

2. Heinrich Ott, *Glaube und Bekennen. Ein Beitrag zum ökumenischen Dialog,* Begegnung, 2 (Basel, 1963), p. 42.

3. Adalbert Hamman, OFM, *Das Geheimnis der Erlosten* (Freiburg im Breisgau, 1954). Translated from the French, this book offers a survey of the entire Scriptures relative to the Redemption in expectancy, fulfillment, and continuation in the Church. This work is especially recommended, particularly in that it provides a very good synthesis of the Protestant and Catholic view of Scriptures. The present author owes much to this work.

4. Denzinger, *Enchiridion Symbolorum,* 32nd ed. (Freiburg, 1963). Reference should be made here to the entire *Decretum super peccato originali,* 787–792; cf. Neuner-Roos, *Der Glaube der Kirche in den Urkunden der Lehrverkündigung,* 3rd ed. (Regensburg, 1949), pp. 224, 225.

5. Cf. Stephan Richter, OFM, "Das Fundament des geistlichen Lebens" in *Der Christliche Sonntag,* XV (1963), p. 47.

6. On the whole question of whether the posting of the theses really took place, cf. Erwin Iserloh, *Luthers Thesenanschlag—Tatsache oder Legende?* (Wiesbaden, 1962). This whole problem, on which Professor Peter Meinhold, the Protestant Church-historian in Kiel, also took a position, can only be mentioned in passing. The question of the factuality of the posting of the theses does not affect our assertions.

7. Cf. Walter Ruff, *Die Thesen von Wittenberg. Eine Einführung* (Berlin, 1952).

3

The Sacrament of Holy Penance

PENANCE IN SALVATION HISTORY

Are Christian penance and the sacrament of penance inter-related or are they mutually exclusive?

To be sure, the Reformation (e.g., Luther's theses) regarded the two as irreconcilably opposed to one another (see the preceding chapter).

Now even in the Old Covenant, sin is not viewed primarily, or even generally, as a private affair between the individual and his God. Because the provisions and mandates of God establish not an order between the individual and God, but rather a covenant of God with His chosen people, so also with sins against that covenant. Israel becomes the people of Yahweh in a very special sense that goes much deeper than the relationship of any other people to God. It was the people as a whole that rejected this covenant when they began to grumble on the journey through the desert, and it was the individual who rejected it as a member of this chosen people when he turned from God to idols, or when he bore false witness, or stole, or broke the bonds of matrimony.

Yahweh's admonition generally applied both to the people as a whole and to the individual member at the same time, especially when He spoke of sin: "Rid thy company of such a plague as this!" (Deut. 13, 6). There was a special ritual for the expiation of the people as a whole as well as for that of the individual. Consider, for example, Leviticus 4, 1ff.: the expiatory sacrifice of the high priest; and Leviticus 4, 13ff.: the expiatory sacrifice of the entire community: "Or perhaps the whole people of Israel has been betrayed into a fault, transgressing the Lord's command unwittingly. If so, when they find out their error, they will bring a young bullock to the tabernacle door in amends," and thus we can come to some appreciation of not only how strongly the idea of expiation was engrained in the minds of the people of the covenant but furthermore how carefully it was brought into action. We should make a special reference here to chapter 16 of the book of Leviticus and to the great Day of Atonement. And now let us pass on to New Testament examples.

Our Lord expressly recommends to his disciples the practice of forgiveness and remission of sins within the community circle: "I promise you, all that you bind on earth shall be bound in heaven, and all that you loose on earth shall be loosed in heaven" (Matt. 18, 18; cf. Matt. 16, 19). In the language of the day, to bind and to loose meant to speak with authority, and in this case to forbid or permit with authority, especially here with reference to the eternal salvation or perdition of man. (That it also implied the binding or loosing of diabolic powers and authorities is of great importance, of course, but it need not concern us here.) The Lord sets up among men an authority which reaches to heaven, i.e., to God Himself. Indeed, God here identifies Himself with the very judgments of the Apostles.

And now we come to the words that John gives us as the Lord's Paschal message in the twentieth chapter of his holy gospel: "Receive the Holy Spirit; when you forgive men's sins, they are forgiven, when you hold them bound, they are held bound" (John 20, 22f.).

These words were spoken on the evening of Easter day. That is the day upon which everything depends, for "if Christ has not risen, then our preaching is groundless, and your faith, too, is groundless" (cf. the very meaningful fifteenth chapter of the first Epistle to the Corinthians). Those who look upon the resurrection of our Lord as a mythical event will also relegate to mythology this commissioning of the disciples on Easter Sunday evening. Now the faithful Christian, whether he be Protestant, Catholic, or Orthodox, will listen carefully to each word of the holy text, *for the Easter gift that the eleven Apostles received from Him who has just risen from the grave is precisely this power and prerogative of forgiving sins:* "When you forgive sins, they are forgiven." It is the same authoritative word that we hear in Matthew 16 and 18. These are plain facts that need no hairsplitting demonstrations. One is at liberty to see this Johannine text as a specific "variant of the binding and loosing tradition" if one wishes.[1] But this does not change the fact that we have received the great gift of peace with God through the forgiveness of sins on Easter day and in connection with the Lord's resurrection. To be sure, it is bound up with the communication or "confession" of sins, for how shall they bind and loose from sins that are not made known to them? Furthermore, it is not everybody who is empowered to bind and to loose, but only the Apostles.

In any case, no sacrament like the sacrament of penance seems to have developed in the centuries that followed. Neither Joseph nor his foster-son Jesus built, in their carpentry shop, the first confessional. On this point, Vorgrimler says, in his highly readable study: "It is historically and theologically false to regard this transition (from the early Church's penitential disciplines to the secret or enclosed confessional form prevailing today) as the distinction between 'public' and 'private' penance."[2] The term *mia metanoia* (penance once) is of decisive significance in early Christianity. In the second and even in the third century, the rigorous practice whereby baptized persons who had lost their baptismal grace of being children of God were admitted only once to the sacrament of penance is based, at least in part, upon the expected immediate return of the Lord (e.g., in the *Shepherd of Hermas*). In the early Church, there was still a consciousness of the true mystery of the thing to which the Christian is called: the mystery of the Lord's death and resurrection and the sealing of the whole on Pentecost, all of which opened up a new era. This consciousness bound one to walk in a new life, and this thought dominated the whole of the Christian's sense of life. It was precisely the reverse—unfortunately—of the consciousness of faith of so many present-day Christians who, after a good and holy confession, maintain their union in grace with Christ only for a short time. One would think that the state of grace were not the norm for Christians! Except for periods of great feasts, they consider themselves outside the communion of grace and "fallen back into the servitude of sin" because of this or that serious sin (which usually means sins against the sixth commandment). This extraordinarily pressing problem must and shall be discussed later on in our study.

We wish to establish here, however, that in the early Church the normal state of the baptized person, one who received the new life, was precisely that of living this fullness of life he had received. Should it have actually happened that he separated himself from the *ecclesia* in a serious way—in the sense of Paul's catalogue of vices (cf. Gal. 5, 19ff. or Romans 1, 29–3; 13, 13; I Cor. 5, 11, etc.)—then the *ecclesia* demanded penance in public. This public act must be regarded as the reaction of the Church or the community of the beloved and elect of God against the guilt they found in their midst. This sin had to be eliminated, and this meant cutting a person off from the community of saints. Not a complete cutting off, for the sinner remained, even as one guilty of sin, a person marked with the seal of the triune God. But the sinner could not take part in the most sacred mysteries—i.e., the communion table of the Lord—until he had performed works of penance and reparation in the form prescribed by the Church. One still had a tangible sense of what Paul said to his community in Corinth about the body which the Church represents: the one life going out from the one Head, the glorified Lord, and streaming through the whole body and each member. Each is a member of this holy organism only so long as its life is in him, only so long as he does not cut himself off from that life through serious sin. In any case, this early community was very clear about what such sin was and meant. There is no doubt that serious sin was known to them, as is apparent from the Epistle to the Corinthians. And there were sins in the early Christian com-

munity which one does not even like to name. But this was
evidently the rare exception. The whole sense of life was
dominated by the idea of the magnificent freedom of being
children of God, by the consciousness of having been baptized into this freedom, and hence the awareness of being a
member of the mystery-filled Body of the Lord (cf. I Cor. 12).

Things changed with time, for not everyone was of the first
generation, not everyone had experienced at first-hand the original events and was awaiting the return of the Lord. There
were mediocre Christians then as there are now, those who
postponed conversion often until they lay on their death-bed.
And not only did they postpone conversion in general, but
even the reception of the sacrament of holy baptism as well
as that of holy penance. The emperor Constantine, who was
baptized only on his death-bed, is an example of this remarkable practice. But on the whole, this age was great in
its direct understanding of Christian reality as well as of sin
and conversion. There was nothing like the secrecy and
covering-up that plagues the interior life of so many Christians in modern times. For the penitent was received in the
midst of the community where he performed his penance
openly in their presence and promised them to amend his
life, trusting in the prayers of the Church in his behalf. The
bishop himself admonished the son or daughter who was
subject to the attractions of a return to the old life of sin—
Paul speaks knowledgeably of "the old servitude of sin."
Taking Christ's place, the father of the community fixed the
forms and time of penance, and after the penance was performed, the reception of the penitent was solemnly executed
with the laying on of hands as a sign of the Church's petition

that the Holy Spirit of God should come to the penitent. All of this made the individual penitent and the participating community vividly aware of what Paul meant with his warning "not to let the utterances of the Spirit be stifled" (cf. I Thess. 5, 19).[3] Our present liturgy on Quadragesima Sunday still breathes something of this spirit of the great rising up to go to the baptismal font and of the spirit of renewal in penance and conversion.

The decisive change from the early Christian practice to our present practices began in the sixth and seventh centuries. The change had to come, with the great numbers of believers —remember that by this time Christianity had been for some three hundred years the state religion—and the mediocrity that necessarily accompanied this growth, but it was also due to a distortion of the principle of "penance once." In any case it becomes a concrete fact with Theodore of Tarsus (named Archbishop of Canterbury in 668). It was in the Irish Anglo-Saxon area that individual private penance was introduced, and it was done by monks. However, in the short span of time up to the eighth century, this practice spread everywhere in the entire continent of Europe. Very soon thereupon, we encounter the regular administration of the sacrament of penance, either in the Lenten season or, in some places, three times in the year. By the twelfth century, annual confession becomes obligatory. The Fourth Lateran Council in 1215 ratified this custom and exacted annual confession at least for those in mortal sin, joining to this the requirement of the reception of the holy sacrament of the Eucharist in the Easter season *"suscipiens reverenter ad minus in Pascha Eucharistiae sacramentum"* (Denz. 437). The same council furthermore required that "this salutary

mandate" (*salutare statutum*) should be announced frequently
in the churches so that no person who failed to comply with
the regulation could have the excuse of ignorance and thus
regard himself as guiltless. The possibility was also recognized
that a person might wish to confess his sins not to "his priest,"
but to an unknown priest. Luke 10, 34, is quoted: the priest
should pour "wine and oil" into the wounds of the sinner with
the greatest care and discretion. This decision of the Fourth
Lateran Council casts significant light on the understanding
and penitential practices of the times, and this was a full three
hundred years before the outbreak of the Reformation. In any
case, one must be careful with the claim that this was an
exclusively negative development, as if there were only a general decay from the bright heights of early Christianity down
to a sort of minimalism and formalism against which Luther
reacted so violently in his day.

We can and must see the working of the Holy Spirit even
in the development introduced by these Irish-Scottish monks
and completed in those definitions of the official Church relating to the "devotional confession" (the very expression
strikes us as impossible!), as Pius XII was to call it in both
Mystici Corporis and *Mediator Dei*.

The words of the Apostle, "The written law inflicts death,
whereas the spiritual law brings life" (II Cor. 3, 6), also apply
with respect to the development of the sacrament of penance.
It would be apostasy if the legacy of the Lord had been betrayed or if man had reduced the holy gifts of God to a mere
formalism or to something even worse.

After this brief historical review of the development of the
sacrament of penance, let us turn now to an important state-

ment of the teaching office of the Church, namely, that of the German bishops who, in 1942, promulgated certain important directions concerning the practice and administration of the sacrament of penance. These directions, which are unfortunately too little known, seem to us to be so relevant for our purposes here, that we have decided to quote them in full.[4] They are as follows:

DIRECTIONS OF THE GERMAN BISHOPS IN 1942 RELATED TO THE PRACTICE AND ADMINISTRATION OF THE SACRAMENT OF PENANCE

A. DOGMATIC PRINCIPLES

1. Since sin and penance are for the Christian directly related to salvation, they must be regarded as belonging not only to the ethical order, but to the religious order in general. It is only from Christ that we really come to understand what the sin of our first parents and personal sin are and mean. Thus even in the light of faith, the arguments against sin, penance, and confession, as well as the difficulties of faithful persons, should be answered straightforwardly and completely.

Sin has its only reality in relation to a personal, holy God. Mortal sin, which is still possible even for the Christian, is thus not merely an infraction of a commandment or a mistake. It is not merely a violation of cult and form, but a self-glorifying and self-exalting "no" to the eternal plan and will of God, a "no" to the call of His love. Sin is the willed and conscious reversal and disturbance of the order of life, a denial of the

loving wisdom of God for the realization of which man has
been lovingly equipped and called by God. Finally, sin is a
"no" to the very essence of God. Now, the sin of the Christian
means—and this makes his sin more serious—the loss of his
life of grace in Christ. It is a reversal of the purpose of the
life of Christ, who wished nothing but to fulfill the will of
His Father even to the point of death on the Cross (Phil. 2).
It is a breach of trust in the obligations assumed with baptism
and confirmation (the indelible seal). It is an injustice and an
attack against the holiness of the Church and her community.

These remarks also apply to venial sin, but only in an
analogous sense. Venial sin is only *contra actum,* not *contra
habitum caritatis,* a halt or straying from the way leading to
God. However, it must be taken very seriously as an offense
against God's holy order and must be rejected and avoided
especially by persons called to be children of God. Reparation
for guilt is made, before men, through conversion and punishment. Before God, however, there is no way for man to make
reparation for his guilt. A fully satisfying reparation before
God for sin became possible only through the God-man when
it was actually effected in the redemptive work of Christ.
Therefore, no conversion (change of heart) or reparation is
possible or efficacious except by virtue of the Cross, since grace
is possible and efficacious only through and in Christ (John
1, 17).

2. God placed upon man the task of developing the powers
and talents that were given him through the natural and
supernatural image and likeness of God. He gave him for this
purpose certain objective norms and laws which are based
directly or indirectly on God's essence. These are experienced

in man's conscience as norms for his behavior. Man must follow the subjectively certain conscience even should it be invincibly mistaken.

This sentence applies universally and without exception. It is implied, however, that man takes the effort to obtain knowledge of the objective norms and to judge the individual concrete case as to its agreement or disagreement with the objective norms known (cf. B, 4, below).

3. The sacrament of penance must be regarded in its dogmatic position together with the other sacraments. In it, there occurs an encounter with Christ of an exceptional kind, namely, the winning back, in a laborious "second baptism," of the life of Christ lost through sin. It is a participation in the Cross of Christ from the special point of view of a benevolent court of justice in cases of sin. It gives expression to its form as a court of justice before the face of the Church by means of the powers of the keys invested in her.

In this way, the dead member wins back the life of Christ, and celebrates resurrection and restoration with Him. The guilt is not only forgiven in the sense that God thinks no more about it. Indeed it is really cancelled and extinguished, so that the Christian is innocent again and new again in grace. Thus the sacrament is a victory of God in man, and the recovery of His honor. For the Christian, it is in a special sense the sacrament of peace (*Pax vobis*). The Council of Trent (Sess. 14, 3) says: "The essence and effect of this sacrament is reconciliation with God." This is why it is common for persons who approach this sacrament with piety to experience, as a concomitant, joy and lightness of heart, and an immense spiritual consolation.

Dogmatic Historical Development

It is an essential and abiding feature of the Church that she has always been concerned about the painful reality of the sin of the Christian. To be a "Christian" does not simply mean to be "redeemed" in the full sense of the word. [These remarks naturally do not imply any limitation on the "definitiveness" of the objective redemptive work of Christ, but refer—as will be clear from the following statements—to the subjective appropriation of that Redemption to the individual, who is always imperfect]. The penitential call of the Church thus always stressed the ideal of Christian holiness as much as the "healing" aspect of the Church through which Christ's salvation is communicated by grace. The Church always regards the sinner (*in peccato gravi*—when in the state of mortal sin) as still a member, albeit a dead member, of Christ's Body, or as a dead branch on the vine. But always he who had good will was able to return to life again through the sacrament of penance.

The act of executing the ecclesiastical power of the keys was always the focal point about which the penitential actions of the penitents—remorse, confession, reparation—turned. Confession is made not merely before God, but before the Church, or, more specifically, before the priest. Ecclesiastical forgiveness, which alone restored one's right to the Eucharist, was in serious cases (*peccata capitalia*) the affair of the bishop or of the priest specifically charged by him for that purpose. An absolutely unforgivable sin has never existed for the Church. The obligation of confession and penance was binding for all serious sins committed after baptism, whether they were public sins or private sins, or even sins of thought.

Certain changes came with time. For example, the early and medieval Church up to the fourteenth century knew a public penance for so-called "crimina capitalia." Alongside this, there was a lighter form of penance for the more commonly occurring sins, namely, the so-called private penance and half-public penance. Indeed up to the late Middle Ages, there was a much greater severity in the penitential practices and in the time they required than is the custom today. The devotional confession as we know it was unknown to the early Church, although its beginnings are seen in the monastic confessions from the time of St. Basil or perhaps Cassian. Regular inclusion of venial sins in confession came with the Irish monastic confession in the seventh century. From this period, however, the Church attributes greater importance to a constant private penance for daily imperfections. Indeed this concern for a deepened conscience necessarily tended to bring about the frequent confession of lesser sins, because the confession itself gave the sacramental means both for an enlightened and sharpened consciousness of guilt and for the removal of the guilt itself. The Council of Trent acknowledged this development, when it said: "Venial sins, which do not cut us off from God's grace and into which we frequently fall, can be confessed. And this can be to our great benefit, and it should not be done with arrogance of any kind, as can be seen from the custom of many God-fearing people. But one can also remain silent and do penance for them with many other salutary means" (Trid. sess. XIV, cap. 5; Neuner-Roos 564; Denz. 899).

This development occurred under the influence of the Holy Spirit and it corresponds to a deepening insight into the fundamental dogmatic truths of Revelation. A return to an earlier stage would be impossible. As a matter of fact, the communion decrees of Pius X have initiated still another stage in this development. In the main, this phase will bring us to a new consideration of the customary frequency of confession and it will assure the Holy Eucharist of a clear, preferential position (not so much a dogmatic as a pastoral position).

The Biblical Foundation

Penance in the Old Covenant. In the Old Testament, the notion of penance is rooted in the powerful idea of God: God the Creator and Lord of all things, God the rewarder of the good and the avenger of the evil. The historical books bear repeated witness to the penance and conversion of individuals as well as of the entire people. The prophetic books provide the overwhelming call to penance of the great Old Testament prophets of God. But it is in the Psalms that we find the richest and most beautiful expression of the realities of penance: the profound sinfulness of man, the cry for redemption, the will to conversion and turning to God, punishment and reparation, justice and mercy. And not only in the *Miserere* and the *De Profundis* and the seven penitential psalms, but the entire psalter is filled with these things. Indeed, it is for this reason that the book of Psalms has become the great song of praise and penitential prayer in the Church's liturgy.

John the Baptist's Call to Penance. In the New Testament, John the Baptist begins his preaching in this way: *Turn away from evil, turn your life to God!* And he points the way to Him who will take upon Himself the penance for the guilt of the world and who alone will redeem mankind from all sin: "Ecce agnus Dei!"

Specifically, he says, in Matthew 3, 2: "Repent, the kingdom of heaven is at hand." The way is open to conversion and repentance. And in Matthew 3, 8, we read: "Come, then, yield the acceptable fruit of repentance" (i.e., works which really indicate conversion). The blessings of penance and the curse of impenitence. Luke 3, 8 demands a change of heart and works of penance. In Matthew 3, 11 and Mark 1, 4, baptism with water is the sense image for conversion and purification which the Redeemer's baptism in the Spirit will complete.

The Lord's Call to Penance. Jesus' message for humanity begins with the same words as the preaching of His Precursor: "From that time onwards, Jesus began to preach; Repent, he said, the kingdom of heaven is at hand" (Matt. 4, 17).

This was the initial preaching of the Lord. Unlike that of the Old Testament and of John, it is a preaching of the "good news" in which Jesus unites the two notions: "Repent, and believe the Gospel" (Mark 1, 15). The groundwork of the call to penance is the same as that established by John, namely, the advent of God's kingdom. This kingdom of God demands full "conversion" of one's thinking and life as is so powerfully expressed later in the Sermon on the Mount.

The call to penance permeates the entire message of Jesus until it resounds in His last words of departure where he charges His disciples to preach, beginning in Jerusalem, to all peoples in the name of the Messiah, the One sent from God, calling them to do penance and to have their sins forgiven (cf. Luke 24, 47). Thereupon He sends down the gift promised by the Father upon His disciples, thus equipping them with strength from heaven.

The call to penance is above all a message of joy in heaven and earth, as is made so clear in the parables of the fifteenth chapter of St. Luke, e.g., the parables of the lost sheep and of the lost drachma, but especially that of the prodigal son, in which Jesus' teaching concerning penance reaches its most perfect expression. But the wonderful doctrine of the sacrament of penance is firmly based upon the Lord's words: "Peace be upon you; I came upon an errand from my Father, and now I am sending you out in my turn. Receive the Holy Spirit . . . when you forgive men's sins . . . !" (John 20, 21–23).

The Apostles' Call to Penance. True to the charge of his Master, Peter called men to penance in all his preaching. In his pentecostal sermon (Acts 3, 19), in the speech of the Apostles before the high council, etc., the thought of penance is always bound up with the suffering and death of the Redeemer.

Paul experienced in his own person the miracle of conversion (Acts 9), and thereupon spoke the words of conversion: "Lord, what wilt thou have me do?" and began immediately to preach penance and turning to God. In his departing words (Acts 20, 21), he says that the one thing which confirms his universal preaching, whether it be to Jew or to Gentile, publicly or in private, is that they should turn to God and believe in our Lord Jesus Christ: "I have proclaimed both to Jew and to Greek repentance before God and faith in our Lord Jesus Christ." In his self-defense before Agrippa, he points out that "first of all in Damascus, then in Jerusalem, then to all the country of Judaea, then to the heathen, I preached repentance, bidding them turn to God, and so to act as befits men who are penitent" (Acts 26, 20).

The thought of penance recurs constantly in the epistles of the Apostle to the Gentiles. In the second chapter of his letter to the Romans, he warns the Jewish Christians of God's anger and counsels circumcision of the heart. In II Corinthians 7, 2–11, grieving becomes conversion, God-pleasing remorse brings about a salutary change of heart as well as seriousness, fear, longing, and reparation. In Colossians 3, he tells us that the conversion of the new man demands discipline and self-denial, but here, too, there is the joy in the Lord. In Hebrews 6, 6, we read his frightening words about the impossibility of a second baptism and the curse of impenitence. And again in Hebrews 6, 9, we hear of the hope in salvation for all who perform works of penance.

We have no records of specific sermons of John the Evangelist. But the strength of his call to penance is clear in the seven epistles to the seven communities in the second and third chapters of the Apocalypse, where the words, like a cutting sword, resound: "Remember how the gift, how the message came to thee; hold it fast, and repent. If thou failest in thy watch, I will come upon thee like a thief; thou shalt never know the hour of my coming to thee." Then John writes of the more gentle solicitation to do penance: "See, where I stand at the door, knocking," but he also describes with harsh realism the terrifying figure of the eternal Judge and the rejection of the impenitent. One phrase from his first epistle is a source of consolation for all who do penance: "If

our consciences condemn us, it is because God is above conscience, and nothing is hidden from Him" (I John 3, 20).

B. GUIDING PRINCIPLES

1. *Education in penance and in the sacrament of penance
must be conceived and carried out as an integral part of religious education.*

a) This education presupposes the fundamental attitude of
Christian faith, the living belief in the almighty and all-holy
God, Lord over all that exists, in Christ, His only-begotten
Son, as the Redeemer and Judge of the living and the dead,
in the Church as the vessel of salvation founded by Christ
and as the salvific community of those who were born of God
in the Holy Spirit.

As a precondition for the correct attitude of conscience and
for a genuine sense of guilt, for acknowledgment of the obligation of penance and of the sacrament of penance, this faith
must be so deeply rooted that it grows into a living fear of and
selfless love for God, and into the consciousness of uncon-
ditioned obligation before His holy will.

b) This education presupposes the basic attitude of Christian morality. The young Christian must come to see the
Christian moral law as the wise expression of God's order of
creation, not as a list of arbitrary "dos" and "don'ts" to which
man must yield. He must see it positively as the law of life
itself for man and humanity.

The young Christian must gain from the figure and message of Jesus Christ the correct picture of God the Father in
His transcendence and greatness and beauty.

In such a basic attitude of Christian faith and morality, the young Christian will see sin as a rupture of the holy ordering of things by God and as an offense against God, as an act against the meaning of life and a denial of the Christian idea and dignity of man, as infidelity and as an act against the holy community in Christ and in the Church. Hence it is above all a question of the fundamental issues of God's honor (*hallowed be Thy name*), God's will (*Thy will be done*), the fear of God (*forgive us our trespasses*), and of God's love (*Father, Thy kingdom come*) becoming alive in our lives. It is a question of forming the young Christian with the life and teaching of Jesus Christ in the full scope of the good news so that Christ's love will penetrate into his whole existence. For he will find, in this basic attitude and in this holy knowledge and love, clear direction and strong answers for every difficulty in life.

2. *True education in penance must respect the inhibitions which the young have, owing both to the nature of youth and to the spirit of the times and their environment.*

a) The young are generally inclined by nature to a superficial, light-hearted spiritual attitude which is quite removed from the notions of guilt and reparation, or penance and conversion. This attitude receives confirmation through the influence of the world with all its irreverence, insolence and thoughtlessness. Moreover, the spiritual currents of the last decades still persist (subjectivism, collectivism, Nietzsche, etc.) with their emphasis on self, on self-glorification and on self-assuredness wherein sin appears as nothing less than an expression of freedom and virility. All this is a reversal of the final terms of man-God relations and of I-we relations, and it is all clearly opposed to personal religion, so much so that it destroys the very spiritual basis for acknowledgment of guilt, need for reparation, and conversion. It is already consciously at work in the child, but it has particularly strong effects in the age of puberty and adolescence.

Certain phenomena which have always worked as obstacles to the attainment of these ends are today even more pernicious than ever. For example, the negative attitude of those in one's closest social environment or in the community in general. Or the confusion caused by witty clichés against sin and confession. We may not overlook the external hindrance caused by overinvolvement in one's professional or working life. And finally there are definite hindrances due to inadequate opportunity to confess, often because the times and schedules of confession are not fitted to people's needs.

Finally we must consider the inhibition which young persons often receive from their experiences in confessing as children. This may come from not having been taken seriously or not having been understood or simply from having been handled incorrectly by confessors. Or it may have arisen from a more or less faulty catechesis or practice of confession in childhood, where a certain amount of formalism and mechanism produces an exaggerated concern for externals and a low esteem for all else. What often remains in the person's thinking about confession is more the mere fulfillment of childhood obligations or the mere technique of confessional procedure and the enumeration of sins, while the essentials of contrition, conversion, turning to God, the freedom and peace of God's children pass completely into oblivion.

b) In the face of these obstacles, due concern must be given to carrying the whole religious education much deeper even from the time of childhood. It must be personally and vitally rooted in the sense of the fundamental Christian attitudes and teachings (see above). The sense for the essential must be opened up.

The young person must be taken seriously in the sacrament of penance. The passing of judgment upon the young person must keep the above-mentioned hindrances and obstacles in mind at all times. The act of confession must be highly esteemed and recognized today as an important work of penance and as an extraordinary expression of good will, religious attitude, and fidelity.

Access to the sacrament of penance must be made easier for the young (cf. below, B, 7).

For the inner attitude toward the sacrament and toward overcoming inhibitions, especially reactions against frequent confession, the positive effects and even the emotional values should be especially stressed, namely, gaining spiritual peace and clarity, knowledge of self and courage before the truth, the strength for overcoming self and the maturing of one's character.

It is also important that the young Christian be led, in all his religious education even from his earliest years, to the proud and joyful consciousness of being "distinct" by virtue of being a "Christian," to conscious religious decisions, to perseverance in his own commitments, to the courage of his convictions in the face of the crowd in all its manifestations, and to fortitude in suffering with Christ.

3. *The Church's teaching concerning penance.*

The Church's teaching concerning penance is made known

in the announcing of Christ's message in preaching and in catechesis. And catechesis should not, especially in this regard, end with childhood. On the contrary, a continuing catechesis of adolescents is essential. Indeed, this should be done formally in religious classes and meetings of young people, but there must also be a personal teaching, explanation and direction at the time the sacrament of penance is actually being administered.

Education in penance must be rooted clearly in the basic teaching of God's lordship and glory and must open the way to the mystery of guilt and redemption, of freedom and reparation, and it must lead to the peace of Christ and to the freedom and glory of being God's children!

Education in penance should center the learner's attention upon the general teaching of the Lord's call to penance and His death of reparation, upon a penitential mental attitude, and upon works of penance. It must then build and develop the teaching concerning the sacrament of penance upon this foundation. *The use of the term "confession" should be suppressed in favor of the more correct expression, "reception of the sacrament of penance."* For in teaching about penance, contrition and conversion should be given more weight than the actual confession or acknowledgment of sins.

In teaching about sin, the notions of sin and mortal sin must be more clearly defined and more firmly impressed upon the conscience.

Both in teaching and in dealing with the penitent, the proper pastoral approach must be deduced from the theological definition of mortal sin (*aversio a Deo,* or turning from God).

Therefore let us have no misuse of the term "mortal sin" because of pedagogical eagerness. We should be deeply serious about all sin, but let us be extremely careful in judgments concerning mortal sin and the state of grace or about the death and life of the soul! (Attention must be directed to the essentials of God's demands and the inner attitude. This applies both to the formation of the individual conscience and to the confessor's judgment of the conscience.)

The Church's teaching on penance (in face of the misapprehensions and the decline of faith which tend to discredit it —cf. B, 2, above) must focus on the "liberty of God's children" and the "gloria Dei."

4. *The formation of conscience.*

The formation of conscience is an essential part of education in penance, indeed in religious education as a whole and in the structuring of a person's life in general. Its aim is the conscientiousness and maturity of the Christian as a free, God-oriented man.

Conscientiousness is the positive striving for clarity in moral thinking and the readiness to obey what one has recognized as the binding will of God.

The full maturity of the conscience is inner strength in conscious, personal decisions in fulfilling God's will in given situations according to His commandments and the teaching of the Church.

Consequently, proper formation of the conscience requires:
a) standing in the fear of God and living in the love of God —and in all this vigilance of the conscience before the eyes of God (cf. B, 1, above).
b) knowledge of the Law in the decalogue and in the deca-

logue's fulfillment in the great commandment of love; further-more, it means living familiarity with the words and figure of Jesus Christ in His message of good news (cf. B, 3, above).

It must be impressed clearly and firmly in the young Christian's consciousness that man is bound in conscience to an objective norm in the divine laws as taught by the Church, and that the Church is called and bound by Christ to state with authority the fundamental laws of morality and to watch over their observance. However, it is true that within this framework, the conscience itself is the dividing rule of moral judgment and action.

The right formation of conscience also requires the exercise or training of the conscience.

As to (a): The training of the conscience for vigilance consists in the daily examination of conscience in the evening prayers (for example, before the Confiteor of compline), in the weekly examination of conscience at the reception of holy communion on Sunday (before the Confiteor at the foot of the altar), and in the thorough examination of conscience before the reception of the sacrament of penance.

It consists furthermore in the habit of questioning one's conscience before judging and acting in important decisions in daily life: "Lord, what wilt thou have me do?" (Acts 9, 6). After the commission of a sin, the questioning of the conscience must be directed particularly to the origin of the sin and its occasions. It should not dwell too much upon the matter of the sin (especially in sins against the sixth Commandment).

As to (b): The judgment of the conscience must be exercised by comparing the law and will of God with the life and will of the sinful man. This can and must be exercised above all in religious classes for young people and in the small, familiar religious circle, using theoretical cases or, what is even better, cases out of the experience and suffering in the life of man and real men. In all these things, the question of the conscience must be put personally. Not "What is commanded or forbidden?" but "What does the Master require of me here and now?" and beyond this, "What, according to the words and person of Jesus Christ, should I best do in order truly to respond to God's honor and love?" For Christ Himself must step into the center of the questioning and provide the decision, or the yardstick for the decision.

Above all, we must seek the inner exoneration of the conscience in perfect contrition. This is all the more true now, when for so many living in the disorders of war or separated from their loved ones, it is the only possible way back to God. One precondition for this contrition is the sharpening of one's judgment concerning sin and, in particular, mortal sin. Correct knowledge and understanding of these things is absolutely indispensable for the formation of a sound conscience, so that this is one of the most decisive points in such exercises.

Furthermore, one must lead and direct the person to the voluntary practice of penance, which means, of course, certain exercises which the Christian performs on his own before confession. "Come, then, yield the acceptable fruit of repentance!" (Luke 3, 8).

The right formation of the conscience must also warn against, and protect the person from, the errors of a faulty conscience, such as the lax conscience, the conscience deafened by the noise of the world and the rush of life, the conscience blinded by the delusions of passion, lying, and self-deception, the conscience which is helpless (even to the point of the horror of scrupulosity) and which never comes to a clear decision or to peace, and the dead conscience which, because of accumulated sins, smothers to the point of complete silence in a godless and prayerless existence.

The formation of the conscience and hence a life of essential piety before God is served by leading the person into tranquility, naturalness, and solitude, all of which the Christian needs again and again in order to come to himself, to his true personality, and to the divine life within him.

5. *The five parts of the sacrament of penance.*

a) *The examination of conscience.* The yardstick for the examination of conscience is, to begin with, the Ten Commandments and the Precepts of the Church, but besides these the exalted demands of the commandment of love in the noble image of Christian man as we find it in the words and figure of Christ in the New Testament.

The examination of conscience should not only prepare for the confessions of sins, but should lead to the clear judgment of oneself before God, so that the young person gains a true perspective on himself in his guilt before God and on his failure to respond adequately to his high calling. Therefore, the primary question put to the conscience before confession should be: "How do I stand in guilt before the living God?" The question of how to confess it must always be regarded as secondary in importance.

The examination of conscience concerns itself not only with the acknowledgment of sinful deeds (actus), but also with perverted sinful attitudes (habitus), with sins of omission, and with everything that the conscientious and positive living of life in Christ does not allow to take place. A re-examination of our customs in preparing for confession according to these principles is a pressing need.

b) *Contrition.* In contrition, the essential question is that of awakening the right consciousness of guilt in sinful actions and in sinful attitudes which can be corrected.

Contrition is the turning of the will from past evil and directing it to God. It is a re-thinking and an inner conversion, a re-positioning of the entire personality which transpires, as does sin, in the will, and which also sweeps the passions into play, expressing itself in tangible feelings, which is good and just.

The Council of Trent defines contrition as: *animi dolor ac detestatio de peccato commisso cum proposito non peccandi de cetero* (Trid. sess. XIV, cap. 4).

Contrition is therefore essentially a looking backward. It is precisely in this honest, even if painful, looking back that the value and salutary power of contrition consists.

The right ordering of the affections is of great significance for moral decisions, the strength of moral motives, and man's overall attitude toward life and reality.

The aim in leading a person to contrition must always be the love of God, which means perfect contrition, and always in relationship to Christ. Prayers or acts of contrition, especially where venial sins are concerned, must reflect true proportion in their wording and thoughts. They must not contain expressions or assertions which offend against the truth or which are psychologically impossible.

As motives capable of inducing contrition and penance in

young people today (those in the adolescent years, but especially those who have advanced beyond these), the following
are cited as worthy of special note: God's greatness and glory,
His justice and His judgment—sin as a contradiction against
the being and meaning of man and as a rupture of God's
holy order—loss of divine childhood—the Cross of Christ and
Christus crucifixus (after the example of so many saints, particularly German saints)—*imago Christi:* our image before
God, our fall from a great calling (cf. the epistles to the
seven communities in the Apocalypse)—*imago Christi:* our
image before men whom we have been called, with Christ,
to save; *salus populi:* guilt before the community, hence penance and reparation for the community—responsibility for
life, etc.

c) *The Resolution* should be concretely realizable in terms
of the young person's present life. He should above all take
up the question of his relationship to the sources of sin, and
then the question of a change of attitude and of avoiding the
occasions of sin. The resolution should go beyond the general
decision "to sin no more," to the positive resolution to follow
Christ especially in that area where one has failed significantly
up to the present, or else in a decisive religious point that is
important in the perfect structuring of Christian life. The
"special resolution" made and followed for a certain period of
time can give good results.

For the confessor, it is an essential principle in the correct
education in penance that he must grow in discretion and
mildness, especially when judging the degree of guilt; but
in the acts of penance demanded, he must be ever more de-

cided, ever more precise, and ever greater in inspiration! These acts or prayers to be performed are often of decisive significance for a person's resolution to change his life.

d) Except when necessary, the *confession* should not be a mere pro forma and schematic recounting of sins, but above all the personal acknowledgment of guilt.

This can only be reached, however, if the person is led, by way of a correct formation of conscience from childhood, to maturity in the independent and authentic judgment of the state of his own soul. To a certain extent even children are already capable of this. The penitent should be held to a short and clear statement of essential facts. The confessor should furthermore give the penitent a genuine opportunity for further expression through a responsive and encouraging word during or at the end of the confession. In the case of frequent confession where the education of the penitent is especially in question, it is generally good to let the penitent speak about the causes of the sin, about his drives and inhibitions deriving from character and personality, about moral contexts and frameworks, and also about his progress in the interior life (in his special resolution), so that such a confession may serve as the basis for authentic spiritual growth.

e) *The penance,* as one of the five essential parts of the sacrament, should be regarded as a sacramental act of reparation in union with the death of reparation of our Lord. Therefore, precisely with the young, the confessor should refer repeatedly to its sacramental character and its symbolic meaning. (The short additional prayer of penance cannot and should not be taken as full reparation or as full satisfaction.)

Hence the conferring of penance must not be uniform and schematic, but should be in some way related to the guilt confessed and adapted to the state of the penitent's soul.

As acts of reparation for sacramental penance, the following should also be considered: a specific period of silent prayer, visits to church or a shrine, readings from Holy Scripture, hearing a sermon. Acts of mortification and charity toward one's neighbor, especially the giving of alms, are also recommended here. For the good of the penitent's conscience, no works of penance should be imposed whose fulfillment is too difficult or too general or indefinite. One should tend rather to the lesser of imposed penances and encourage the penitent to religious exercises and good works which he can take freely upon himself and which he can determine on his own. The young in particular should be led to such voluntary acts of penance for the sake of God's honor, for the increase of religious moral strength, and in reparation for our people.

6. *Education toward a penitential mentality and toward penitential prayers and works.*

The basis for education toward a penitential mentality has been mentioned in sections B, 1 and B, 3 above. It should be given special attention in the penitential seasons of the liturgical year and should always lead to the correct Christian attitude toward penance, namely, a conscious participation in Christ's Cross.

For penitential prayer, the act of contrition should be supplemented by other prayers, as has always been the teaching of the Church. Christians must be led to the daily and frequent use of short penitential prayers such as: "Lord, have mercy on me, miserable sinner!" (Luke 18, 13), or "My

Jesus, have mercy!" or "Most Sacred Heart of Jesus, have mercy on us!" or "Mary, refuge of sinners, pray for us!," etc. And they should further be led to longer penitential prayers such as the Psalms, *Miserere* or *De Profundis,* or the Prayer to the Five Most Precious Wounds. And this is where an intelligent introduction to the use of indulgenced prayers and practices can be made.

As to penitential works, the Christian must give first place to the conscious acceptance of the crosses and sufferings sent by divine providence in his daily life. This means, for example, difficulties in one's vocation or work, corporal suffering, or spiritual hardship. The voluntary, painful yet joyful bearing of such crosses as participations in Christ's Cross is the apex of Christian penance.

Then come voluntary works such as prayers, fasting, giving of alms, etc. Examples of *prayer* are holy hours, the Way of the Cross, the rosary, the prayers at the end of the litany of All Saints, or other small exercises. Examples of *fasting* include all exercises of mortification and self-denial, whether of a corporal or spiritual nature, and also abstention from legitimate pleasure. Because of the false ideas of humility and the negative esteem for life current in our day, the notions of self-denial and mortification must be clarified again in the light of the Cross (Matt. 16, 24) and of life (John 10, 10). The *giving of alms* means all exercises of Christian charity in the corporal and spiritual works of mercy, and at the head of the list comes the actual giving of material goods to those who need them. All this should be practiced from early youth and in a measure that can be felt as a sacrifice.

In no exercise or act of penance should the Christian dis-

play a dismal, depressed, or sad face. Rather it is the brave,
hopeful, and joyful bearing of the redeemed Christian that
should be the foundation here and which should be clearly
expressed in the outward appearance of the person (Matt. 6,
16; II Cor. 9, 7).

It is important to lead the Christian from the performance
of prayers and works of penance for his own sins to the
thought and deed of reparation for the general guilt of his
people and all Christianity, to vicarious satisfaction with
Christ and all the saints. Precisely today in the midst of the
indescribable immorality in world affairs, there is great salutary significance in leading the youth of the Church to
thoughts of reparation and to prayer and works of reparation
even to the point of martyrdom.

It is important for religious education in penance and penitential works that the young Christian be led, by means of
secular education, to a greater severity of life, self-discipline,
perseverance in difficult things, and manliness.

7. *The administration of the sacrament of penance.*

In order to ease the way for the young person over the
various obstacles he frequently has to contend with (B, 2
above), the following measures should be taken:

The time-schedule for confession must be adapted to the
prevailing working and living conditions of a community and
it must be arranged so that a long waiting-in-line can be
avoided as much as possible. The place of confession and the
confessional itself should afford a certain amount of solitude
and privacy. For young men, it is a considerable easing of
things if only men confess on one side of the confessional,
and only women on the other. Regularly, and at suitable hours

(not too infrequently), a larger number of confessors must be made available.

The leading of the young people to this sacrament depends more upon the bearing and behavior of the confessor than upon anything else. A respectful and respect-commanding manner, an understanding judgment of and serious concern for human affairs, consciousness of responsibility, kindness in showing the way to a truly better life, and personal dedication to Christ mean, for the young, the difference between a person to be followed and one to be avoided.

The confessor's exhortation must turn essentially on the issue of the penitent's conversion, and it must be neither too long nor too general, paying rather special attention to the state of the penitent's soul and to his religious habits. It should center upon the words and will of Christ, and lead to new and increasingly deeper religious decisions. It should appeal to the honor and courage of the young Christian and should always send him away with a word of real joy and something of the peace of the Lord!

Still, it is not the confessor's talk, but his absolution which is essential, and therefore the uttering of the formula of absolution should always be performed in a slow and dignified way, and with a visibly solemn movement of the hands. For this is the real liturgical act, and something of its solemnity should be conveyed, through the senses, to the spirit of the penitent.

CONCLUSIONS

The preceding episcopal directions constitute an authentic set of spiritual exercises, indeed in a certain sense they are a modern Magna Charta for the practice of penance and the administration of the sacrament of penance. It is not important that these directions happen to be dealing primarily with the situation of youth, seeking to provide them with clear principles and guidelines for their particular situation.

Indeed, these episcopal directions can give genuine help to all Christians. They constitute an important statement of the teaching office of the Church. In truth, Christians of all communities who are concerned with genuine penance and with the correct execution or re-appropriation of the holy sacrament of penance will find in these directions much to profit by.

We can draw the following conclusions from the episcopal statement:

1. Penance is, in a very real sense, the consummation and substance of the Christian's life.[5] He is called throughout his entire life to follow Christ in penance, and this penance is what makes his life as a Christian. Either he understands the Master's message in this way, or he misunderstands it completely. Indeed, properly understood from this viewpoint, even Luther's "simul justus et peccator" proves to have profound meaning and value.

2. Out of this basic attitude toward penance, the holy sacrament of penance and its proper execution come as its mature and necessary fruit. The Christian no longer sees in this sacrament a burden or merely a duty, but the Easter gift of the risen Lord. In the prophetic expectation of the Old Covenant as in the good news of the New Testament, and especially in the fulfillment of our Lord's message, the Chris-

tian will learn what penance really means and what "gift of God's grace in Jesus Christ" has been shared with us in the sacrament of penance. It is important that this be conveyed when preparing the young for first confession as well as when instructing youth during the years that follow. But it would appear that the sacrament of penance and the very idea of penance as the basic attitude for Christian living continue to be minimized in our preaching and instruction, as they have been for a long time.

3. The main stress must fall upon a genuine and all-embracing formation of the conscience. This formation must be oriented to the Ten Commandments as the fundamental groundwork of the Christian life, or, in the words of Johannes Pinsk, "as the way to the glory of Christian living."[6] But even more, this formation must be oriented toward the person of the Lord Himself, toward His guiding words, His signs, His actions, and especially toward His selfless and self-sacrificing love depicted so well in His exemplary washing of feet.

It is much more a question of formation of the attitude of the conscience than of the correct procedure in specific "cases." To be sure, it will always have to come down to specifics, but it will always tend to consider these in view of the whole, and will *never* revert to casuistry of any kind. The formation must progress patiently from level to level: in the family, at home, in preparation for first confession, in the deepening of moral awareness during puberty and adolescence, and so on to mature manhood and womanhood.

As serious as individual mortal sins are, one must never lose sight of the fact that the principal issue in the Christian formation of conscience is that of the overall turning to God and the general hatred for and abstention from sin. The ultimate aim must be the "magnificent freedom of being children of God."

We urge the reader to refer again to the words in the above-quoted episcopal directions that concern the Catholic understanding of conscience in general and the occasional decisions of conscience in particular.

The great commandment of love which is basically the one and only commandment stands, together with the glory of God, squarely in the center of the formation of conscience. A narrowing or overstressing of the Sixth Commandment shifts the accent which God, the founder of all order, established and which Christ renewed and deepened.

The Christian formation of conscience does not get caught up in a "situation morality," but rather keeps a clear view on the principles of the growth and maturing of the moral personality. It pays due attention to the necessary stages of a "morality of development," and it considers itself bound by the Lord Himself when He said: "It is by endurance that you will secure possession of your souls" (Luke 21, 19).

The Christian formation of conscience traces all moral and human effort back to the basic law of love. In this perspective, the *peccatum veniale,* the venial or "wound" sin, also falls into place. Mortal sin is the total, conscious, and voluntary refusal before God the Father who reaches out to us in the crucified, glorified, and returning Christ. Venial sin is to love too little, something which one could bring up to normal if one wished, if one is zealous and vigilant, and not remiss.

4. Contrition is an interior process. Through it, the penitent gets free of himself, and is no longer lost in things and sin-

ful drives. It is through contrition that the penitent makes his way to the foot of the Lord's Cross. "Lord, you know everything, but you also know that I love you," prays Peter and every sinner in the sincerity of his heart. He places his sin entirely in the mercy of God, drops his eyes in shame with the tax-collector: "Lord, have pity on me, a sinner!" and yet he knows, with the trusting certainty of the prodigal son, that his Father is waiting for him. Because the Christian is always only beginning with God, his contrition accompanies him at every moment, for he knows that he falls daily far behind God's love, and perhaps even renounces that love completely on occasion.

The Christian knows the difference between perfect and imperfect contrition.[7] Imperfect contrition has a strong element of fear in it, while perfect contrition is rooted soundly in the love of a child for his Father. For the proper education in penance and confession, it is important *always* to strive for perfect contrition. This should not be too difficult. The whole religious life of the Christian centers in fact around the loving deeds of God who calls us in His Son-become-man, calling us especially from the Cross. Either Christ is the center of the Christian's life, or it has no center! Many examples of the breakdown of Christian institutions are due to the fact that Christians often stand on the periphery without ever really coming into contact with the living Lord. Contrition must be the all-embracing act of love and must always grow more intense as the basic attitude of the Christian's life deepens. Learn to say that you suffer from the smallness of your love and that you are ever setting out into a deepened manifestation of this your love! This is the contrition of the Christian!

5. The true penitent does not enter, with his resolution, into an unnatural posture about which he lacks conviction. He knows what constitutes danger for him and he knows his own weaknesses, but above all he knows God's gracious mercy, which is always new. Full of humility and confidence in God's grace, he reconsiders the words from Lamentations: "God knows it shall be remembered, and with sinking of the heart; gage there can be none other of remaining confidence. His be the thanks if we are not extinguished; his mercies never weary; Hope comes with each dawn; art thou not faithful, Lord, to thy promise? Heart whispers, The Lord is my portion; I will trust him yet" (Lamentations 3, 20–24).

To be sure, man makes the new beginning through his sincere will to improve. But he knows that he can do nothing beyond this, and that he can only persevere in this will to be a better person if and because he is supported by grace. With Paul, he knows of God's wisdom and direction: "My grace is enough for thee; my strength finds its full scope in thy weakness" (II Cor. 12, 9). In spite of all the sincerity of his effort and his ever new and good resolutions, the Christian knows about *fragilitas humana*, his weakness and proneness to danger. Indeed, it is precisely this awareness which makes him profoundly humble and merciful toward *every* other person. In the secret depths of the heart, every man has experienced how God writes straight even on crooked lines, as the old Spanish proverb says.

Because it is always today for God,[8] man dares to begin anew every day, trusting, above all else, in the grace of God. The grace of always beginning afresh is one of the most pleasant of Christian realities.

6. The confession of sins must be fitted, as much as possible, to the personal contingencies of the penitent. A profound wisdom is expressed in the conditions laid down by the Church for the valid reception of the holy sacrament of penance. There must be no infringement on the natural freedom of the human person.

Tilmann never tires of reminding us that the clear structuring and formation of the conscience is more important than the confession itself. Nevertheless, even with the best will, much will necessarily remain "schematic" and "mechanical." But, above all, is it not the heart of the person confessing that is decisive, and not his possibly superficial or even perhaps dull and emotionless expression? Much more frequently, the problem lies with the confessor, especially on those days when he is in heavy demand. On such days, it is hardly possible for any penitent to confess his sins in real peace and to have a really personal talk with his confessor. Haste and routine must be kept far from the holy sources of life which the sacraments in general are, and especially from the sacrament of holy penance.

The pastoral talk and spiritual direction may be made as parts of the actual administration of the sacrament of penance, although they may be given at another time and place, apart from the sacrament. We should also distinguish clearly between the actual confession and the instruction which is always a form of spiritual direction, and the pastoral talk in the strict sense. Naturally, there are always many persons with genuine problems who wish to bring these up precisely within the confines of confession, for the seal of confession often constitutes the condition without which many would not dare

to reveal their difficulties and would otherwise keep them
tightly guarded in the lonely silence of their hearts. With all
our love and esteem for the early Church and all our efforts
to re-emphasize precisely the public character of sin and
penance, we still have to keep in mind the changed life-
situation of the modern Christian. Probably there should be
much more opportunity for discussion "in the field," where
pastoral reality unfolds, such as, for example, takes place
within the framework of the "Open Door" experiment.

We are touching here in part upon the whole problem area
of "confession and psychoanalysis." This short study will
hardly permit us to do much more than to mention the problem and to point up the issues it entails. To this end, we refer
the reader to the highly recommended book of Max Thurian
of Taizé, *Confession,* where he discusses the psychoanalytical
approach to spiritual and moral phenomena as well as the
psychological analysis of sin. The Christian life, Thurian
maintains, always involves interior weakness and hardship and
exterior scorn and persecution. The Christian should not
merely lament the conditions of his life, but analyze and accept them and put them to use for the glory of God.[9]

We can only touch here upon the whole complex of questions. Thurian at least provides us with some very essential
perspectives in his enlightening study.

7. A penitential problem of particularly pressing nature
today is that of the performance of penance. Indeed, we are in
serious need in this area, if not sometimes at an utter loss.
Specifically, one's entire life after confession ought to be
marked by genuine penance. But it is not so important that an
exterior penance should be imposed on the penitent as that the

penance should mean, at least symbolically, a new beginning in life. Little is accomplished by imposing upon the penitent the recitation of this or that decade of the rosary or the praying of the litany of the Holy Name of Jesus. For since this does not correspond rationally or imaginatively to the sin to be amended, it can hardly be considered authentic penance (such as in the case of serious sins against charity which are, unfortunately, often taken all too lightly and which are commonly confessed, and heard by the confessor, as "only" venial sins).

And the vast area of work and professional life? Can this area really be so insignificant in the spiritual life that it is almost universally and entirely ignored in the formation of conscience and in the performance of penance in one's practical life? The penitential task to be performed should be worked out in terms of the great commandment of love and of the actualization of charity in one's daily activities, whatever they be.

An example of genuine penance would be for a doctor to dedicate the eight weeks following confession to the study of a fundamental work in his field of specialization. Or for anyone who offends social justice to give specific and tangible assistance to some social institution or work. The Old Testament idea of tithes is not at all so remote from all this. In any case, the "penance given" must come to grips with the concrete person in his good will and it must touch the nerve-point that gets him started in the direction of real amendment of his life.

These sketchy and wholly fragmentary reflections are aimed only at bringing the problem into view, a problem which is doubtless one of the most important for a re-evaluation of the sacrament of penance.

Notes

1. Cf. Herbert Vorgrimler, "Bussakrament," in *Handbuch theologischer Grundbegriffe,* I (Munich, 1962), p. 209. On the whole question, cf. also Karl Rahner, "Vergessene Wahrheiten über das Bussakrament," in *Schriften zur Theologie,* II (Einsiedeln, 1955), pp. 143–185; same author, the article "Bussakrament," in *Lexikon für Theologie und Kirche* (Freiburg im Breisgau, 1958), Vol. II, pp. 826–838.

2. *Loc. cit.,* p. 209.

3. Cf. J. A. Jungmann, "Bussriten," in *Lexikon für Theologie und Kirche* (Freiburg im Breisgau, 1958). Our present work is primarily concerned with the theological content and pastoral orientations of these directives, and not with controversial questions concerning the history of dogma.

4. *Führung zu Busse und Sakrament: Katechetische Blätter* 72 (1947), pp. 25–29 and 84–92.

5. Cf. on the whole matter the extremely important work of Klemens Tilmann, *Die Führung zu Busse, Beichte und christlichem Leben,* Klarung und Wegweisung, 3 (Würzburg, 1961).

6. Johannes Pinsk, "Der Christliche Sinn der Zehn Gebote," in *Lebendiges Zeugnis,* II (1953).

7. Express reference is made here to the important studies of my honored teacher, Rev. Dr. Valens Heynck, OFM, on *contritio* and *attritio* and the doctrine of penance in general in Duns Scotus and Bonaventure. Cf. *Franziskanische Studien,* 23 (1941), pp. 65–90; 36 (1954), pp. 1–81; 38 (1956), pp. 39–65 and 150–176.

8. Cf. Roger Schutz, *ibid.,* especially the chapter "Christus das Feuer seiner Liebe in uns entzünden lassen." See also Stephan Richter, "Hodie—Heute," in *Der Christliche Sonntag,* 13 (1961), p. 25.

9. See Max Thurian, *Confession* (Naperville, Allenson, 1958).

4

Confession Viewed by Protestant Christianity

LUTHER

If we were to say in a word how Luther looked upon confession, we should say very simply that he loved confession. As a matter of fact, he was deeply devoted to it and he promoted it diligently everywhere during his entire life.

"The shame and infamy that a person should strip himself before another human person, inform on himself and deride himself, what a precious piece of the Holy Cross! Oh, if we only knew what punishment is prevented by such voluntary blushing, if we only knew how merciful it makes God when man denies and humbles himself for His honor, we would exhume the practice of confession and travel a thousand miles to confess our sins," writes the reformer Martin Luther.[1]

And in another place: "If you are poor and miserable, then go and make use of health-bringing physics. He who really suffers with his misery and difficulty will have such a desire for medicine that he will actually run to it with joy. But they who neither acknowledge its powers nor come of their own accord should be allowed to go their way. They should be advised, however, that we do not regard them as Christians. And so we wish to teach how excellent, how choice, and how consoling a thing confession is, and we warn everyone not to despise such a thing so good and dear in relation to our needy condition. If you are a Christian, then you need neither my urging nor the Pope's command at all, but you will urge yourself and you will ask me to let you share such a good. But if you insist upon despising it and upon continuing to live unconfessed in your sins, then we must conclude that you are no Christian and that you should not enjoy the sacrament. For you despise what no Christian should despise, and you thereby make it impossible for yourself to have forgiveness for your sins. And this is furthermore a sure sign that you also despise the Gospel.

"In conclusion, we do not want to be forced. But with him who neither listens to nor follows our preaching and admonishment, we shall have nothing to do, and he shall have nothing to do with the Gospel. If you were a Christian, you should be glad to walk a hundred miles without being called, but rather you would yourself call us. For the calling should be reversed in these things: it is you who are free to command us. We force no man, but we allow men to force us just as we are forced to preaching and to dispensing the sacraments. Therefore, when I admonish men to confession, I do nothing more than exhort them to be Christians. If I get you to be a Christian, then I have also got you to confess your sins. For whoever desires to be a devout Christian and to be free of his sins and to have a peaceful conscience thereby has the proper hunger and thirst to snap at the bread much as the hunted deer burns with hunger and thirst in Psalm 42, 3: 'As the hart panteth after the fountains of water, so my soul panteth after thee, O God.' In other words, how we ache and long for God's word, or for absolution and sacrament. Don't you see, it would be to teach correctly about confession to let people love and lust after it, to let them seek and run after it more than we ourselves would wish. Let the papists trouble and martyr themselves and others, despising and closing themselves off from such a treasure. But let us lift our hands to praise and thank God that we have come to such knowledge and grace."[2]

On the basis of such texts, which incidentally could be multiplied, there can be no doubt that Martin Luther took from his Catholic background a love for the sacrament of penance and upheld its practice both in his own life and in his preaching to others. In fact, confession was nothing less than a self-evident reality in his thinking as a Christian. Many will be surprised at Luther's identification of Christian life with the holy sacrament of penance. It is in fact definitely known that the deeply devout Luther regularly received the paschal sacrament of peace from his friend and spiritual director, Bugenhagen. Indeed, these words, which would be a worthy utterance for any Christian, are credited to Luther: "The devil would have strangled me long ago, had I not this secret refuge of confession." Throughout all the phases of his life, he regarded confession as a gift, in the truest sense of the word, direct from Christ, and it was one of the things which made him happiest.

In the light of all this, it seems really inconsequential to dispute whether or not Luther really considered holy confession as one of the seven holy sacraments. Also of little real

significance is the question of whether he was subject to
fickleness in his theological understanding, or actually took
different positions in different periods (following certain experiences and impressions). According to the theologian of
Taizé, Max Thurian, Luther stands unmovable in favor of
the sacramentality of confession.[3] According to Laurentius
Klein, Luther takes a "wavering position" in the question of
its sacramentality. The year 1520 is obviously an important
turning point in Luther's life and in his general understanding of the substance of the faith he had received. "It is
extremely questionable whether statements made by Luther
after 1520 which still refer to confession as a sacrament may
really be taken to mean that he began again to count confession among the sacraments in the strict sense."[4] Obviously the
first two of Luther's theses (reread the text already given
above) already attempt to separate confession from penance.
But it does not appear too important to this writer that Luther
did or did not, throughout the years after 1517, display a
constant conviction of including penance among the sacraments of the Church, or that he was now certain, now un-
certain about it, or that he sometimes rejected it entirely as a
sacrament in the "catholic" or universal sense.

To this writer, of far greater significance is the certain
evidence we have of Martin Luther's having actually held
fast, throughout all the phases of his active life, to the *practice*
of confession in the Catholic sense. Yes, in the Catholic sense.
For he practiced the confession and acknowledgment of sin
in sorrow and humility before a fellow human who returned
him the service of uttering God's word and who was a
"minister of the mystery of God." (To be sure, this was only

in a very limited sense. The question of consecrated priest-hood and of the universal priesthood cannot be considered in any detail here.) Above all, the reformer's personal practices seem to this writer to be of immense importance. As a matter of fact, he confessed according to regular "Catholic" practice. His great objection, and it constituted for him a genuine scandal, was that of being under obligation to confess. The great Innocent III had opened the Fourth Lateran Council in 1215 with the words from St. Luke 22, 15: "I have longed to share this paschal meal with you before my passion," and then the Council proceeded to make the minimum require-ment of "confession in the Easter season" for those in mortal sin solemnly binding upon the universal Church.[5] Luther, who was so deeply concerned with, and who so vehemently postulated, "the freedom of the Christian person," was thoroughly repelled by this obligation even in his years as a monk in an Augustinian monastery. And then came the prac-tice connected with all this, to wit, the commerce in indul-gences which is so hard for us to understand today. Add to this the danger that threatens everything that is holy, and especially holy confession, namely, the tendency to mecha-nism, formalism, and to the mere fulfillment of pure com-mands.

There must have been many occasions then, as there are also today, to recall the words of the Lord: "This people does me honor with its lips, but its heart is far from me. Their worship of me is in vain, for the doctrines they teach are the commandments of men" (Matt. 15, 8). Our Lord is quoting here from Isaias 29, 13, evidently to show how deeply inclined man is to turn his personal and holy relationship with God into a mere performance of obligations at best. But God is concerned with the heart. Luther is thoroughly understandable in his rejection and criticism of a penitential practice that runs counter to the holy word of God. But didn't Luther strain the bow of "freedom of the Christian person"? Was he not himself horrified at how misunderstood he was? It became common practice to go to the Lord's Supper without even thinking of receiving the sacrament of holy penance as a demonstration of humility, although it is true that the sacrament certainly continued to be widely available in spite of its distortion. We can still read Luther's sermons in which his every word shakes with anger over the fact that his freedom of the Christian person was so wrongly interpreted. The fact is that Luther's doctrine of freedom makes it possible to remove precisely whatever one finds to be unacceptable and burdensome in the holy sacrament of penance, so that one ends up with the view that a general attitude of contrition is sufficient. Even Luther found it impossible to tip the scales with his deep belief in confession, his understanding of conversion and the turning of the heart, his *metanoia,* his preaching of a penitential attitude and of sincere confession, and his insistence upon the necessity of personal absolution. Thus he in fact sowed the seed for a development that he himself neither wanted nor foresaw, but at times had to accept to his horror, namely, that confession as he loved it and practiced it and preached it was threatening to fall into total disuse. Add to this the emotional stamp in Luther's temperament that often caused him to pass over essentials even in his preaching on the sacrament of penance, and in fact in his utterances regarding the idea and the administration of the sacrament.

In all, we find that we must agree with Laurentius Klein's comprehensive position, which in turn refers us to the assertions made earlier by Böhme: "No Protestant Christian can be hindered from regarding confession as a sacrament (thus far Böhme). But the reverse of this is also true, namely, that no Protestant Christian can be hindered from regarding confession, by reason of Luther's theology, as not one of the sacraments. This holds true for the just estimation of the various teachings concerning confession that have been proposed in the course of history and that have invoked Luther's writings in their support." Most important is the general recognition of this assertion by Klein: "The question ends, of course, in the problem of the true interpretation of Luther. But the question lacks the dynamism in Protestant theology that it has in Catholic thought because Protestant theology ascribes much less significance to the sacraments in general than they receive in Catholic theology."[6]

This brings us to a complex of questions which far exceeds the limits of this small study, to wit, that of how the Lutheran "alone" on the one hand and the dictum of "word and sacrament" on the other are to be understood in view of the whole. Does Luther not postulate an "alone" where the holy word of God proposes the copulative "and" or even an "as well as"? Does not the calling of the Church into question necessarily also put a holy gift of God, as confession was and remained for Luther, into the danger of being inadequately understood? Or putting it another way, does not the whole gift of the grace of salvation intended for us by Christ in His Church run the risk of falling into dissolution and misunderstanding, of being reduced to partial aspects if we do not go all the way,

in spite of all obstacles, to a *credo ecclesiam?* For we can
have the Lord, and the forgiveness of our sins through Him,
only in His Church, in His and her word and sacrament, in
her order as founded by Him.

OTHER REFORMERS
AND LATER PROTESTANTS

Penance is no sacrament for Calvin, for "the Lord instituted
no outward ceremony for the purpose of strengthening our
faith," and furthermore there is no divine promise, which
would in fact be the only valid foundation for the sacrament.
"And really, the promise of the power of the keys does not
make a special office out of absolution, but exclusively out of
the preaching of the Gospel. . . ." These highly apodictic
statements of the Geneva reformer are cited in Max Thurian's
above-mentioned book.[7]

Calvin based his position upon the lack of matter in the
sacrament of penance. To be sure, this very sacrament is quite
special with regard to the problem of matter. Indeed, the
problem presented itself much earlier with the Scotists, and it
was Thomas Aquinas and the Council of Florence that
worked out a clear answer in the notion of "quasi-matter"
which manifests itself in the acts of the penitent—contrition,
resolution, humble confession, etc. Calvin oversimplifies
when he reasons that where there is no matter, there is also
no sacrament. And with this pseudo-reasoning, he drops
confessional penance altogether. But Luther's own followers
pose and sharpen the question of whether Luther himself,
with all his personal esteem for and practice of confession in

his life, was able to keep this "spring of living water" clean and pure. Or is it true that, as many scholars claim, the Reformation began in the confessional?[8] Does the reformer (and his followers after him) perhaps project something into confession which he then, because of a subjective problem such as scruples or over-anxiety, did not find there? The "how can I war against a merciful God?" at the beginning probably developed, in its many ramifications in religious practice, into much stronger forms than is usually assumed. Can we really regard it as normal that Luther, even after 1517, at times confessed and received absolution daily? Or, putting it more radically, did he really find for himself what he advocated so loudly for others, namely, the freedom of the Christian person? And do not his "scripture alone" and his "by grace alone" contain in fact a dangerous tendency to onesidedness? Does he not actually overstress God's transcendence, of which he is so sure, and to a great extent overlook the creature man, who he says is inexplicably called by that transcendent Being?

He tells us that we live in these paradoxes by pure grace, and that this grace is a call which can and must have its response. Still, he tells us that it can also echo unheard in the misuse of our freedom. In fact, we can even set ourselves against it with all our means! Who would deny that precisely this often actually occurs? It is certainly tragic that especially with Luther's followers these unclear points in his theology, bound up as they were with unsolved personal problems, took such negative developments precisely in the question of penance and confession. One cannot blame Luther's followers for taking and practicing certain principles more radically and unilaterally than Luther perhaps intended. Calvin surely did this in his own way, and so also did Luther's collaborator Karlstadt. At Christmas, 1521, Karlstadt invited the people of Wittenberg to a celebration of the Lord's Supper without confession before. Two thousand accepted his invitation. In actual practice, Luther's dictum, "You do not have to confess" became for many: "You do not need confession." This was evidently the real act of separation from Rome. At the same time, we can well assume that Karlstadt saw and thought and made a theological and pastoral judgment something like this: Is not the table to which the Lord invites the "just" and especially the sinners from the highways and byways precisely *the* sign of divine forgiveness, divine benevolence, and divine grace? Indeed, can there be a more beautiful and more fitting sign? Here, surely, is the *verbum visibile* of forgiveness, the visible pardon of God. Who needs anything more? Had Karlstadt not understood his teacher perfectly when he concluded that absolution and Holy Communion were only two different forms for guaranteeing and "adapting" God's forgiveness to our conditions? Could one not also speak of a purely eucharistic form of absolution instead of the hitherto exclusive and so troublesome acquittal from past sin based only upon honest confession, contrition, and humility?

It is very easy to understand the thoughts and conclusions of Calvin, Zwingli, and here Karlstadt. When one truth of salvation is considered in complete separation from another, when one mystery of salvation is not seen and evaluated with others in view of the whole, such conclusions and consequences come of necessity. When, for example, the event of the Last Supper on Holy Thursday evening is not oriented to the Easter gift of the risen Lord ("Whose sins you shall forgive, they are forgiven them") and seen as such in deep joy and thankfulness as parts of one unmerited and unmeritable gift of "God in Christ Jesus," such conclusions as those drawn by Karlstadt could not even be avoided. Luther was horrified. He never wanted this. He rushed from Wartburg to Wittenberg to restore order. He delivered one of his Lenten sermons precisely on confession, and this theme was to preoccupy him repeatedly in the future. He remains constant in exhorting his faithful, and especially his collaborators, assuring them that "you do not have to confess; rather you may confess." In spite of all his personal troubles, in fact because of them, confession is and remains for Martin Luther always a great comfort, and never a thorn in his side. Repeatedly he takes up "this second plank after the shipwreck" (*secunda post naufragium tabula*).[9] Was Karlstadt aware of what Paul, in I Corinthians 11, said to his community in Corinth, and thereby to all the faithful who wish to come near to the Lord's Supper, when he warned them about approaching the Holy Eucharist unworthily? With all his esteem (or anyone's, for that matter) for the "freedom of the Christian person," it is certain that there are sins which exclude from the Holy Eucharist until they have been acknowledged in contrition and humility before the Church's ministers of God's forgiveness, i.e., until they have actually been absolved. The peace of the risen Lord of Easter is communicated by men appointed by the Lord so that the sons and daughters of the Lord, liberated thus from sin and guilt, can celebrate with their Lord the holy paschal feast which is no longer that of the Old Covenant of promise, but of the New Covenant of fulfillment and liberation, that of God's utter kindness and humanity and grace. Karlstadt's breaking away from confession and communion could only have disastrous effects.

DEVELOPMENTS UP
TO THE TWENTIETH CENTURY

Luther no longer determined the subsequent developments, as much as he tried, for example, with his treatise, "Short Exhortation to Confession," written in 1529. It had an extremely entreating tone: "Therefore if I exhort you to confess your sins, I do nothing more than exhort you to be a Christian." And again, when he says: "Yes, I would rather bear the Pope's tyranny of fasting, ceremony, vestments, serving trays, capes and whatever else I could stand without doing violence to my faith, than have confession taken from Christians."[10]

Luther was deeply disturbed by the already well advanced state of things. He could no longer even slow it up, and it continued to gain ground. In place of the personal acknowledgment of sins, there was substituted a general, more or less informal admission of sin, and sacramental confession fell into disuse. All his imploring and exhortation accomplished nothing. He was as one crying out in the desert. "The institution of confession began to slide away, and the efforts of the Church authorities to hinder the avalanche with outside means now only succeeded in bringing the Protestant practice of confession into internal decay." For Luther's "double preparation" for the Holy Eucharist, namely the examination of personal belief and private confession, was only an external means for disciplining the Church, and it was incapable of healing the internal disturbances in which she was languishing.

"And so obligatory confession, which had been driven out the front door, came back in by the rear door," writes the author quoted above, Oskar Planck, in his "Protestant Confession Manual."[11] We also have an interesting page from Goethe, where he gives us not only his own experience regarding confession, but that of his whole age as well, in his *Poetry and Truth*:

I found my good will and my efforts in this important matter paralyzed even more by a dry, spiritless routine, as I was supposed to approach the confessional even more frequently now than before. [He had just written of religious instruction.] To be sure, I was conscious of my many shortcomings, but of no serious faults, and this very consciousness diminished even those faults of which I was aware, because it referred me to the moral strength which lay within me and which was finally to rule, by resolution and perseverance, over the Old Adam. We were taught that we were much better than the Catholics precisely because we had nothing particular to acknowledge in the confessional and that it would not even be good if we did have anything serious to confess. This latter did not suit me right. For I had the most singular religious doubt which I would gladly have straightened out, had I the opportunity.

Since this was not to present itself, I planned out a confession for myself which, in expressing my situation, stated in general terms to an understanding man what I was forbidden to say in detail. But as I entered

the old Discalced Carmelite church and approached
the peculiar barred closets in which the priests were
accustomed to sit during this act, as the bellman
opened the door and I found myself now enclosed in
the small room with my spiritual grandfather, and as
he welcomed me with his weak nasal voice, every light
in my spirit and heart suddenly went out, the words I
had memorized perfectly for confession could not find
their way to my lips, and I nervously opened up the
book I had in my hands, reading therein the best short
formula which was so general that anyone could have
spoken it in perfect composure. I received the absolution and left, feeling neither warm nor cold, went the
next day with my parents to the Lord's table and de-
ceived myself for a few days, as was well fitting after
such a holy act.[12]

Later in life, Goethe was to remark that "Aural confession
should never have been taken away from men." Christians
were to suffer deeply from having lost this great liberation
from sin and guilt. Man lives in a dialogue, and wishes to
communicate. Indeed, he must communicate, if he is to avoid
repressions. Our Lord knew very well why He instituted His
Easter gift, the sacrament of penance, essentially as a dialogue.
Martin Luther knew this and appreciated it as only very few
have, but he was unable to transmit this understanding and
appreciation to the generations that followed him. It broke
down more and more as time passed. What a deep longing
for the seven holy sacraments, especially for the personally
executed sacrament of penance, personal confession with

personal acknowledgment of sins and personally spoken absolution, comes through in Goethe's words in the seventh book of the second part of his *Poetry and Truth:* "Now here (in confession) the Christian has, in the endless confusion into which he is driven by the conflict between natural and religious imperatives, a marvelous expedient for the confiding of one's deeds and misdeeds, one's shortcomings and doubts to a worthy man ordained specifically for that purpose and who knows how to quiet a person, how to admonish and strengthen and discipline a person with penalties that are also symbolic, and who finally is able, by absolving the person's guilt completely, to restore the person's happiness and to give him back the original chart and form of his humanity, washed pure and clean."

Goethe is evidently profoundly convinced that his entire life would have taken a radically different course, had he had, in Luther's words, "the private refuge of confession." The "autonomy of the conscience" so loudly proclaimed by the Enlightenment must have thrown many into profound spiritual desolation, loneliness, and absence from God. For if the Lord, who knows best the interior of man, makes such an exalted gift of grace to His disciples, man can hardly turn down such a gift of God, to suit his own taste or whim, without doing serious harm. This singular *mixtum compositum,* part inquiry (if not, indeed, consultation) and part general courtroom for accusation, even part "Eucharistic examination" for the determination of orthodoxy before the reception of the Holy Eucharist, and in itself an authentic sacrament, was destined to die out. In the beginning, people were being examined individually, but this soon became too much, and one began to examine and admonish them in groups. But "with that, confession was completely neglected and mechanized," observes Planck. How logical that Spener, for example, saw "the greatest burden of the office" in the administration of confession.[13] And should we wonder at his deacon Schade, who also directed perhaps the most pointed argument against confession, as is so evident even from the title of his significant publication of 1696, "I Sought Help from Men and Found None," where he writes: "Let him praise it who will! I say: confession-box, Satan-box, fire-pit!" Hans Asmussen comments on this whole situation with no excess of words: "Pietism robbed us of confession!"[13] And Planck adds to this: "Yes, but it gave us confessors. And if we see it rightly, it was necessary to remove that hybrid idea which issued forth from a false development of the Lutheran Church before a form of confession conforming to the Gospel could emerge anew."[13]

Prince Friedrich III wasted no time in removing, in 1698, all obligation to individual confession—at least in the remarkable form mentioned above. From that time on, the confession which Luther had desired and preserved at all costs, in spite of occasional misunderstandings, was replaced in the national churches by the general confession of the whole community. It became a solemn and rare exception for someone to ask for private confession, and even then it was not granted except after express and persistent requests. Schade instituted, in a community of Berlin, the example of a "universal confession," which consisted of a challenging penitential sermon, examination of conscience in common, and an equally common absolution.

The pietistic pastors Christoph Blumhardt and Wilhelm Löhe were the harbingers, in the middle of the last century, of the fundamental renewal that we are witnessing in our century. Both reintroduced private confession in 1843, one in Möttlingen and the other in Neuendettelsau, each of which came to be regarded as important centers of religious life and activity. Earlier, in 1837 in fact, the deeply devout Löhe had published his *Confession and Communion Book for Evangelical Christians,* which went into its ninth edition in 1919.

Others worthy of note were Harms in Hannover, Vilmar in Hessen, Scheidel in Schlesien, etc. Löhe's principle was: "The worst private confession is better than general confession." Claus Harms insisted that "the proper way to the altar goes through the confession-box." But these were only lone voices crying out in the desert.

The Pastoral Conference of Dresden in May, 1856, at which representatives of the churches of Saxony, Bavaria, Hannover, Württemburg, and Mecklenburg participated, was called with a view to restoring order in general pastoral matters, but it was not able, even with its various "canons touching upon confession and absolution," to effect any changes worthy of note. The daily press published the official acts of the conference, and all was quite tranquil, but soon came violent protests from all sides directed to the church leaders, and even to the king as *Summus Episcopus.* Everyone feared the re-institution of obligatory confession. In the *Augsburger Zeitung* of the time, we read that "without doubt the opposition is in the majority," which reflects the atmosphere of Munich, Nürnberg, Kempten, Lindau, and other cities of southern Germany. Laurentius Klein comments on the whole situation that "with the death of men of action, the whole movement died out."[14] The breakthrough to a restoration of personal confession did not take place, even though such confession continued to be practiced individually here and there even up to the turn of the century. Despite their general failure, we can regard with deep appreciation and respect the efforts of those who attempted to resuscitate it. They were the precursors of the development which our generation is witnessing and experiencing, or, better yet, actually originating and shaping. For the Church of sacraments is being newly discovered. It is, to be sure, the Church of the Word. But it is also the Church of the Sacrament, or, to put it in its most absolutely exact terms, *the* Sacrament.

REDISCOVERY OF CONFESSION IN PROTESTANT CHRISTIANITY TODAY

This movement for the restoration of confession cannot be regarded as developing in isolation. On its deepest level, it is part of the phenomenon of the renewal of religious orders and congregations,[15] and an essential element of all this is the longing for sacramental reality in general. The writer can still remember perfectly how astounded he was to read the list of topics in the program of the Evangelical Week in Flensburg just after the war, for among those topics was that of Evangelical Confession. Then in Kiel in 1948, Hans Asmussen delivered a lecture on this subject which this writer has never forgotten. For that which had been maturing in theological understanding and practice, and precisely in the area of personal confession, in the quiet of the Fraternity of St.

Michael (Michaelsbruderschaft), and since 1931 in the Chapel of the Cross in Marburg, and since even earlier in Berneuchen by Brandenburg, now suddenly, after the total collapse of 1945, broke out into public view in academic circles, Evangelical Weeks, and especially in Church conferences such as those of Frankfurt and Munich. What is being practiced especially in the Evangelical-Reformed cloister at Taizé (near what was once Cluny) both in theology and in the administration of the holy sacraments, especially in the celebration of the Eucharist and of personal confession, is attracting an ever broader circle of friends and disciples, and it can be justly regarded as a miracle of God for our time. As early as 1936, W. Stählin published his book, *The Confession of the Individual Christian,* and O. Planck, also a Brother of St. Michael, published his *Evangelical Confession Booklet* in 1956. From the theological viewpoint, the most profound and mature of all the numerous Protestant publications on confession is in this writer's opinion Max Thurian's *Confession.*

Among the movements related to the rediscovery of confession in the Protestant community, we wish to single out the practical pastoral activities current in our day. Personal confession is definitely finding acceptance in Protestant communities. To be sure, in line with the structure of the Lutheran Church in general, this naturally depends to a large extent, if not exclusively, upon the theological leaning of the pastor involved. But happily one does meet pastors everywhere today who are connected with the St. Michael's Fraternity, who do practice personal confession, and who attempt to form their parishes according to their thinking in this regard. Unfortunately, broad areas are still closed to such pastors. It is astound-

ing to see the theological and practical earnestness with which
these pastors go about their task. Recently, this writer was
himself invited to collaborate in setting up a five-member
team for a conference on "Confession from the Catholic
Viewpoint." An initial wave of sound enthusiasm which the
writer had the pleasure of experiencing in the Evangelical
Conference in Frankfurt seems subsequently to have yielded
before hard-headed considerations about a "spreading" of
personal confession. In the Eleventh Evangelical Church
Conference in Dortmund on "Living with Conflicts," in July,
1963, personal confession stood more or less in the background. Why? That is a good question, for this Church Conference departed in many respects from its immediate predecessors.[16]

But it nevertheless appears that in small groups everywhere
a new love for personal confession is making itself seen and
felt. Such movements of grace do not lend themselves—thank
God—to statistics. But one can say, and without exaggerating,
that we stand at the beginning of a new Spring with respect
to confession in the Protestant world. We can add, indeed
we must add, that every Catholic can only rejoice, honestly
rejoice, over the seriousness of pastoral efforts as well as of
personal practice among their separated brethren in this direction, and he should learn from them that formalism and
obligatory confession have been known, at least in one case, to
spoil the pleasure of confession for whole generations of
Christians. The personal concern and the truly existential
efforts of many Evangelical circles to move toward a really
personal confession—remote from all routine and cliché—is
a call to every Catholic who loves his faith and life and

believes in the holy sacraments! We can shower one another
with the richest gifts. Why is it that we don't do it? Or if we
do, why not more intensely? Why not convene in small circles
with responsible pastoral direction to talk with one another
about the holy sacrament of confession, about the true content and meaning of the holy Word of God, about the formation of the Christian conscience, about our practical religious
and moral living and so many more things? I hope I never
hear any one say again that the Church is not yet ready! If
I do, I must conclude that we are less catholic than our
Church Fathers at the Vatican Council in Rome and the
observers included—or better, less catholic than all the Christians from East and West who convened in such clear brother-
liness in Rome during the four years of Vatican II.

The important point with respect to the rediscovery of the
holy sacrament of penance lies no doubt in a deepening of
theological perspectives. In reading the contemporary Protestant literature on the subject of confession, one finds that it is
almost universal practice to begin with Luther. And this is
surely not enough! As nowhere else, it seems to me that the
alpha and omega in this problem consists in delving into
God's holy Word. Scripture alone! Referring to what has been
said above, it is quite clear that Luther and his followers could
be the right point of departure, yet how difficult the inter-
pretations of Luther's books have been and still are![17] It
would seem that Protestant and Catholic biblical theology
have great common tasks precisely with respect to the holy
sacrament of penance. Many special questions such as those
of hereditary sin and personal sin, the relationship between
baptism and penance, the formation of conscience, even the

difficult question of "satisfaction," concern both Churches. Is it possible that in spite of the biblical movement and the liturgical renewal with all their marvelous fruits, a genuine renewal of confession has not taken place among Catholics? Is it possible that discussion of our so-called "devotional confession" (again that horrible expression!) has distracted us from more essential matters?

Metanoia: Christian penance and confession, is a call and a task for each and every one of us.

These considerations have been intended as a small contribution toward the realization of our task, and perhaps as a help towards a new understanding and deeper love for penitential things.

"If thou knewest what it is God gives!" (Our Lord to the Samaritan woman, John 4, 10).

Notes

1. Erich Roth, *Die Privatbeichte und die Schlüsselgewalt in der Theologie der Reformatoren* (Gütersloh, 1952), p. 147. He quotes Wolfgang Böhme, *Beichtlehre für evangelische Christen* (Stuttgart. 1956), pp. 44–45.

2. Böhme, *loc. cit.*, pp. 104, 105.

3. Thurian, *loc. cit.*

4. Cf. Laurentius Klein, *Evangelisch-lutherische Beichte. Lehre und Praxis,* Konfessionskundliche und kontroverstheologische Studien des J.-A.-Möhler-Institutes, V (Paderborn, 1961), pp. 54ff. The reader is referred most emphatically to this significant and fundamental work.

5. Hubert Jedin, *Ecumenical Councils of the Catholic Church* (New York, Paulist Press).

6. Klein, *loc. cit.*, p. 57, note 267; cf. also pp. 248–249, and Böhme, *loc. cit.*, p. 59.

7. *Thurian, loc. cit.*

8. Klein, *loc. cit.*, pp. 162ff.

9. Council of Trent. sess. XIV.

10. Georg Siegmund, "Die Beichte in der protestantischen Kirche," in *Theologie und Glaube*, 53 (1964), pp. 1ff.; he quotes here Böhme and Klein, *loc. cit.*

11. Oskar Planck, *Evangelisches Beichtbüchlein* (Stuttgart, 1957), pp. 29ff.

12. Goethe, *Dichtung und Wahrheit*, Part II, Book 7.

13. Planck, *loc. cit.*, pp. 33–34.

14. Klein, *loc. cit.*, pp. 212ff.

15. Lydia Präger (editor), *Frei für Gott und für die Menschen. Evang. Bruder- und Schwesterschaften der Gegenwart in Selbstdarstellungen* (Stuttgart, 1959). Also Stephan Richter, "Neuentdeckung der Orden in der evangelischen Christenheit," in *Der Christliche Sonntag*, 14 (1962), pp. 45–47; also by Richter, "Stationen einer ökumenischen Frankreichfahrt," *ibid.*, 14 (1962), pp. 93–95 and 101–102.

16. Stephan Richter, "Kirchentag in neuer Form? Rückblickende Notizen zum 11. Evangelischen Kirchentag 24.–28. Juli, 1963," in *Ordo Socialis*, 11 (1963), Vol. 4.

17. Cf. here Klein, *loc. cit.*, pp. 248–250.

Appendix:
Texts Relevant to Penance

THE WORD OF GOD

THE DECALOGUE

And thus he spoke: I am the Lord thy God, it was I who rescued thee from the land of Egypt, where thou didst dwell in slavery. Thou shalt not defy me by making other gods thy own. Thou shalt not carve thyself images, or fashion the likeness of anything in heaven above, or on earth beneath, or in the waters at the roots of earth, to bow down and worship it. I, thy God, the Lord Almighty, am jealous in my love; be my enemy, and thy children, to the third and fourth generation, shall make amends; love me, keep my commandments, and mercy shall be thine a thousand-fold.

Thou shalt not take the name of the Lord thy God lightly on thy lips; if a man uses that name lightly, he will not go unpunished.

Observe the sabbath day and keep it holy, as the Lord thy God has bidden thee. Six days for drudgery, for doing all the work thou hast to do; when the seventh day comes, it is a sabbath, a day of rest, consecrated to the Lord thy God. That day, all work shall be at an end, for thee and for every son and daughter of thine, thy servants and serving-women, thy ass, too, and thy ox, and all thy beasts, and the aliens that live within thy city walls. It must bring rest to thy men-servants and thy maid-servants, as to thyself. Remember that thou too wast a slave in Egypt; what constraining force the Lord used, what a display he made of his power, to rescue thee; and now he will have thee keep this day of rest.

Honor thy father and thy mother, as the Lord God has bidden thee; so shalt thou live long to enjoy the land which the Lord thy God means to give thee.

Thou shalt do no murder.

Thou shalt not commit adultery.

Thou shalt not steal.

Thou shalt not bear false witness against thy neighbor.

Thou shalt not covet thy neighbor's wife.

Thou shalt not set thy heart upon thy neighbor's house or lands, his servants or handmaids, an ox or ass or anything that is his. (Deuteronomy 5, 6–21)

THREE PARABLES OF GOD'S MERCY

The Parable of the Lost Sheep. When they found all the publicans and sinners coming to listen to him, the Pharisees and scribes were indignant; Here is a man, they said, that entertains sinners, and eats with them. Whereupon he told them this parable: If any of you owns a hundred sheep, and has lost one of them, does he not leave the other ninety-nine in the wilderness, and go after the one which is lost until he finds it? And when he does find it, he sets it on his shoulders, rejoicing, and so goes home, and calls his friends and his neighbors together; Rejoice with me, he says to them, I have found my sheep that was lost. So it is, I tell you, in heaven; there will be more rejoicing over one sinner who repents, than over ninety-nine souls that are justified, and have no need of repentance.

The Parable of the Lost Coin. Or if some woman has ten silver pieces by her, and has lost one of them, does she not light a lamp, and sweep the house, and search carefully until she finds it? And when she does find it, she calls her friends and her neighbors together; Rejoice with me, she says, I have found the silver piece which I lost. So it is, I tell you, with the angels of God; there is joy among them over one sinner that repents.

The Parable of the Prodigal Son. Then he said, There was a certain man who had two sons. And the younger of these said to his father, Father, give me that portion of the estate which falls to me. So he divided his property between them. Not many days afterward, the younger son put together all that he had, and went on his travels to a far country, where he wasted his fortune in riotous living. Then, when all was spent, a great famine arose in that country, and he found himself in want; whereupon he went and attached himself to a citizen of that country, who put him on his farm, to feed swine. He would have been glad to fill his belly with husks, such as the swine used to eat; but none was ready to give them to him. Then he came to himself, and said, How many hired servants there are in my father's house, who have more bread than they can eat, and here I am perishing with hunger! I will arise and go to my father, and say to him, Father, I have sinned against heaven, and before thee; I am not worthy, now, to be called thy son; treat me as one of thy hired servants.

And he arose, and went on his way to his father. But, while he was still a long way off, his father saw him, and took pity on him; running up, he threw his arms around his neck and kissed him. And when the son said, Father, I have sinned against heaven and before thee; I am not worthy, now, to be called thy son, the father gave orders to his servants, Bring out the best robe, and clothe him in it; put a ring on his hand, and shoes on his feet. Then bring out the calf that has been fattened, and kill it; let us eat, and make merry; for my son here was dead, and has come to life again, was lost, and is found. And so they began their merry-making.

The elder son, meanwhile, was away on the farm; and on his way home, as he drew near the house, he heard music and dancing; whereupon he called one of the servants and asked what all this meant. He told him, Thy brother has come back, and thy father has killed the fattened calf, glad to have him restored safe and sound. At this he fell into a rage, and would not go in. When his father came out and tried to win him over, he answered his father thus, Think how many years I have lived as thy servant, never transgressing thy commands, and thou hast never made me a present of a kid, to make merry with my friends; and now when this son of thine has come home, one that has swallowed up his patrimony in the company of harlots, thou hast killed the fattened calf in his honor. He said to him, My son, thou art always at my side, and everything that I have is already thine; but for this merry-making and rejoicing there was good reason; thy brother here was dead, and has come to life again; was lost, and is found. (Luke 15)

THE GREATEST COMMANDMENTS

One of the scribes heard their dispute, and finding that he answered to the purpose, came up and asked him, Which is the first commandment of all? Jesus answered him, The first commandment of all is, Listen, Israel; there is no God but the Lord thy God; and thou shalt love the Lord thy God with the love of thy whole heart, and thy whole soul, and thy whole mind, and thy whole strength. This is the first commandment, and the second, its like, is this, Thou shalt love thy neighbor as thyself. There is no other commandment greater than these. And the scribe said to him, Truly, Master, thou hast answered well; there is but one God, and no other beside him; and if a man loves God with all his heart and all his soul and all his understanding and all his strength, and his neighbor as himself, that is greater than all burnt-offerings and sacrifices. Then Jesus, seeing how wisely he had answered, said to him, Thou art not far from the kingdom of God. And after this, no one dared to try him further with questions. (Mark 12, 28–34)

THE BEATITUDES

Jesus, when he saw how great was their number, went up on to the mountainside; there he sat down, and his disciples came about him. And he began speaking to them; this was the teaching he gave. Blessed are the poor in spirit; the kingdom of heaven is theirs. Blessed are the patient; they shall inherit the land. Blessed are those who mourn; they shall be comforted. Blessed are those who hunger and thirst for holiness; they shall have their fill. Blessed are the merciful; they shall obtain mercy. Blessed are the clean of heart; they shall see God. Blessed are the peace-makers; they shall be counted the children of God. Blessed are those who suffer persecution in the cause of right; the kingdom of heaven is theirs. Blessed are you, when men revile you, and persecute you, and speak all manner of evil against you falsely, because of me. Be glad and light-hearted, for a rich reward awaits you in heaven; so it was they persecuted the prophets who went before you. (Matt. 5, 1–12)

THE SEVEN PENITENTIAL PSALMS

Psalm 6

Lord, when thou dost reprove me, let it not be in anger; when thou dost chastise me, let it not be in displeasure. Lord, pity me; I have no strength left; Lord, heal me; my limbs tremble; my spirits are altogether broken; Lord, wilt thou never be content? Lord, turn back, and grant a wretched soul relief; as thou art ever merciful, save me. When death comes, there is no more remembering thee; none can praise thee in the tomb. I am spent with sighing; every night I lie weeping on my bed, till the tears drench my pillow. Grief has dimmed my eyes, faded their lustre now, so many are the adversaries that surround me. Depart from me, all you that traffic in iniquity; the Lord has heard my cry of distress. Here was a prayer divinely heard, a boon divinely granted. All my enemies will be abashed and terrified; taken aback, all in a moment, and put to shame.

Psalm 31

Blessed are they who have found their faults forgiven, their transgressions buried deep; blessed is the man who is not guilty in the Lord's reckoning, the heart that hides no treason. While I kept my own secret, evermore I went sighing, so wasted my frame away, bowed down day and night by thy chastisement; still my strength ebbed, faint as in mid-summer heat. At last I made my transgression known to thee, and I hid my sin no longer; Fault of mine, said I, I here confess to the Lord; and with that, thou didst remit the guilt of my sin. Let every devout soul, then, turn to thee in prayer when hard times befall; rise the floods never so high, they shall have no power to reach it. Thou art my hiding-place, when I am sore bestead; songs of triumph are all about me, and thou my deliverer.

Friend, let me counsel thee, trace for thee the path thy feet should tread; let my prudence watch over thee. Do not be like the horse and the mule, senseless creatures which will not come near thee unless their spirit is tamed by bit and bridle. Again and again the sinner must feel the lash; he who trusts in the Lord finds nothing but mercy all around him.

Just souls, be glad, and rejoice in the Lord; true hearts, make your boast in him.

Psalm 37

Thy reproof, Lord, not thy vengeance; thy chastisement, not thy condemnation! Thy arrows pierce me, thy hand presses me hard; thy anger has driven away all health from my body, never a bone sound in it, so grievous are my sins. My own wrongdoing towers high above me, hangs on me like a heavy burden; my wounds fester and rankle, with my own folly to blame. Beaten down, bowed to the earth, I go mourning all day long, my whole frame afire, my whole body diseased; so spent, so crushed, I groan aloud in the weariness of my heart. Thou, Lord, knowest all my longings, no complaint of mine escapes thee; restless my heart, gone my strength; the very light that shone in my eyes is mine no longer.

Friends and neighbors that meet me keep their distance from a doomed man; old companions shun me. Ill-wishers that grudge me life itself lay snares about me, threaten me with ruin; relentlessly their malice plots against me. And I, all the while, am deaf to their threats, dumb before my accusers; mine the unheeding ear, and the tongue that utters no defense. On thee, Lord, my hopes are set; thou, O Lord my God, wilt listen to me. Such is the prayer I make, Do not let my enemies triumph over me, boast of my downfall. Fall full well I may; misery clouds my view; I am ever ready to publish my guilt, ever anxious over my sin. Unprovoked, their malice still prevails; so many that bear me a grudge so

wantonly, rewarding good with evil, and for the very rightness
of my cause assailing me. Do not fail me, O Lord my God,
do not forsake me; hasten to my defense, O Lord, my only
refuge.

Psalm 50

Have mercy on me, O God, as thou art ever rich in mercy;
in the abundance of thy compassion, blot out the record of my
misdeeds. Wash me clean, cleaner yet, from my guilt, purge
me of my sin, the guilt which I freely acknowledge, the sin
which is never lost to my sight. Thee only my sins have
offended; it is thy will I have disobeyed; thy sentence was
deserved, and still when thou givest award thou hast right on
thy side. For indeed, I was born in sin; guilt was with me
already when my mother conceived me. But thou art a lover
of faithfulness, and now, deep in my heart, thy wisdom has
instructed me. Sprinkle me with a wand of hyssop, and I
shall be clean; washed, I shall be whiter than snow; tidings
send me of good news and rejoicing, and the body that lies
in the dust shall thrill with pride.

Turn thy eyes away from my sins, blot out the record of
my guilt; my God, bring a clean heart to birth within me;
breathe new life, true life, into my being. Do not banish me
from thy presence, do not take thy holy spirit away from
me; give me back the comfort of thy saving power, and
strengthen me in generous resolve. So will I teach the wicked
to follow thy paths; sinners shall come back to thy obedience.
My God, my divine Deliverer, save me from the guilt of
bloodshed! This tongue shall boast of thy mercies; O Lord,

thou wilt open my lips, and my mouth shall tell of thy praise. Thou hast no mind for sacrifice, burnt-offerings, if I brought them, thou wouldst refuse; here, O God, is my sacrifice, a broken spirit; a heart that is humble and contrite thou, O God, wilt never disdain. Lord, in thy great love send prosperity to Sion, so that the walls of Jerusalem may rise again. Then indeed thou wilt take pleasure in solemn sacrifice, in gift and burnt-offering; then indeed bullocks will be laid upon thy altar.

Psalm 101

O Lord, hear my prayer, and let my cry come unto thee. Do not turn thy face away from me, but lend me thy ear in time of affliction; give me swift audience whenever I call upon thee. See how this life passes away like smoke, how this frame wastes like a tinder! Drained of strength, like grass the sun scorches, I leave my food untasted, forgotten; I am spent with sighing, till my skin clings to my bones. I am no better than a pelican out in the desert, an owl on some ruined dwelling; I keep mournful watch, lonely as a single sparrow on the house top. Still my enemies taunt me, in their mad rage make a by-word of me. Ashes are all my food, I drink nothing but what comes to me mingled with tears; I shrink before thy vengeful anger, so low thou hast brought me, who didst once lift me so high. Like a tapering shadow my days dwindle, wasting away, like grass in the sun!

Lord, thou endurest forever, thy name, age after age, is not forgotten; surely thou wilt bestir thyself, and give Sion redress! It is time, now, to take pity on her, the hour has come. See how thy servants love her even in ruin, how they water her dust with their tears! Will not the heathen learn reverence, Lord, for thy glorious name, all those monarchs of the earth, when they hear that the Lord has built Sion anew; that he has revealed himself there in glory, has given heed to the prayer of the afflicted, neglects their appeal no more? Such legend inscribe we for a later age to read it; a new people will arise, to praise the Lord; the Lord, who looks down from his sanctuary on high, viewing earth from heaven, who has listened to the groans of the prisoners, delivered a race that was doomed to die. There will be talk of the Lord's name in Sion, of his praise in Jerusalem, when peoples and kings meet there to pay him their homage.

Here, on my journey, he has brought my strength to an end, cut short my days. What, my God, wilt thou snatch me away, my life half done? Age after age thy years endure; it was thou, Lord, that didst lay the foundations of earth when time began, it was thy hand that built the heavens. They will perish, but thou wilt remain; they will all be like a cloak that grows threadbare, and thou wilt lay them aside like a garment, and exchange them for new; thou art unchanging, thy years can never fail. The posterity of thy servants shall yet hold their lands in peace, their race shall live on in thy keeping.

Psalm 129

Out of the depths I cry to thee, O Lord; Master, listen to my voice; let but thy ears be attentive to the voice that calls on thee for pardon. If thou, Lord, wilt keep record of our iniquities, Master, who has strength to bear it? Ah, but with thee there is forgiveness; be thy name ever revered. I wait for the Lord, for his word of promise my soul waits; patient my soul waits, as ever watchman that looked for the day. Patient as watchman at dawn, for the Lord Israel waits, the Lord with whom there is mercy, with whom is abundant power to ransom. He it is that will ransom Israel from all his iniquities.

Psalm 142

Listen, Lord, to my prayer; give my plea a hearing, as thou art ever faithful; listen, thou who lovest the right. Do not call thy servant to account; what man is there living that can stand guiltless in thy presence? See how my enemies plot against my life, how they have abased me in the dust, set me down in dark places, like the long-forgotten dead! My spirits are crushed within me, my heart is cowed. And my mind goes back to past days; I think of all thou didst once, dwell on the proofs thou gavest of thy power. To thee I spread out my hands in prayer, for thee my soul thirsts, like a land parched with drought.

Hasten, Lord, to answer my prayer; my spirit grows faint. Do not turn thy face away from me, and leave me like one sunk in the abyss. Speedily let me win thy mercy, my hope is in thee; to thee I lift up my heart, show me the path I must follow; to thee I fly for refuge, deliver me, Lord, from my enemies. Thou art my God, teach me to do thy will; let thy gracious spirit lead me, safe ground under my feet. For the honor of thy own name, Lord, grant me life; in thy mercy rescue me from my cruel affliction. Have pity on me, and scatter my enemies; thy servant I; make an end of my cruel persecutors.

GUIDE FOR AN EXAMINATION OF CONSCIENCE*

THE FIRST COMMANDMENT: I, the Lord, am thy God. Thou shalt not defy me by making other gods thy own.

What do I fear above God? Failure? The future? Hardship? A war? Old age? Death?

Have I denied my faith for human respect? Have I esteemed human opinion above God's judgment? Have I really loved God above everything else? Or have my affairs and my possessions, my home, my money, or my career been more important to me than the Lord, my God?

Am I in the grips of a passion?

Have I exalted any human creature to the level of a god in any way? Is my family my all and my everything even to the point of taking up the place in my heart that is due to God alone?

On what do I place my trust? On what do I let my life depend? On my ability? My connections? Do I believe in "fate" or chance?

Do I live thoughtlessly, without foundation or purpose?

Have I, in those moments when God seemingly left me without help, abandoned my trust in Him? Have I believed God capable of overcoming adverse circumstances and contrary wills and of winning to His purposes even the hearts of those who resist Him?

* From the official brochure "Hymns and Texts" distributed at the Eleventh Evangelical Church Conference at Dortmund.

THE SECOND COMMANDMENT: Thou shalt not take the name of the Lord thy God lightly on thy lips; if a man uses that name lightly, the Lord will not acquit him of sin.

Have I spoken God's holy name only with reverence, or have I used it irresponsibly, in curses, or in foul language?

Have I spoken lightly of holy things, of the divine service, of the Bible, or the Church? Or have I listened silently when others did the same in my presence?

Have I been faithful and fervent in prayer and in petitions for heavenly help? Have I engaged in fortune-telling, sooth-saying, or the like?

Have I let myself be charmed or conjured away by anyone? Do I let myself be influenced by horoscopes?

THE THIRD COMMANDMENT: Remember to keep the Sabbath Day holy.

How would an objective observer qualify the way I pass my Sundays and my free time?

Do I hear and read God's Word gladly, or merely as a routine? Do I seek the society of living Christians? Do I listen to God in moments of silence, or do I avoid the question of God by throwing myself into work and pleasure? Do I visit, in the spirit of God's holy Word, the aged, sick, and needy persons in my surroundings with a view to helping or consoling them, or of reading God's Word to them?

THE FOURTH COMMANDMENT: Honor thy father and thy mother; so shalt thou live long to enjoy the land which the Lord thy God means to give thee.

Have I shown gratitude to my parents both in word and

ready deeds? Have I given them some joy? Have I prayed for them?

Have I looked down on them or been ashamed of them? Have I borne the idiosyncrasies of their old age with love and understanding, or have I let them feel my indifference or even my lovelessness?

Have I been insolent toward my parents? Have I contradicted them? Have I made them angry or sad, so that they became excited or even sick?

Have I remembered that I must render an accounting to God for all persons entrusted to my care?

Have I cared for my parents in the spirit of Christ's love —for their spiritual life too? Have I always had enough time for them?

THE FIFTH COMMANDMENT: Thou shalt do no murder.

Have I brought about or caused the death of a human person? Have I killed an unborn child, or contributed in any way to such a death? Have I harmed anyone's health of soul or body?

Have I been careless with my own health?

Have I endangered my own life or that of others in traffic or otherwise?

Have I brought corporal or spiritual help to the poor, the oppressed, those in temptation or in danger? Or am I indifferent to their needs? Do I lack the spirit of sacrifice? Have I always tried to see and love Christ in my neighbor—even in my enemy? Or have I been exclusive, touchy, or ungrateful in thought, word, or deed?

Have I been ready to make the first move toward reconciliation of personal hostilities?

Do I have reverence for all life in nature?

THE SIXTH COMMANDMENT: Thou shalt not commit adultery.

Am I fully aware that I am responsible to God for my body?

Do I have secret imperatives in the area of sex that cause me particular trouble? Are my thoughts and desires chaste?

Have I pursued unchaste conversation or told double-meaning jokes? Have I done everything to bring about a dignified and clean atmosphere in my surroundings?

Have I been clear and decided in every temptation, or have I played with temptations? Have I cut myself off decisively from bad influences (bad films, books, pictures, etc.) and from dangerous acquaintances?

Do I respect the inviolability of my neighbor both before marriage and outside of marriage? What of my own marriage? Whom do I blame first for offenses against its sacredness?

Am I always ready to be the first to forgive?

Have I been faithful in my marriage—in thought, word, and deeds? Have I entertained any unpermitted relationships with persons outside my marriage—possibly only in secret, in thought, or perhaps only a spiritual relationship?

Am I completely dedicated to my marriage-partner? Am I absolutely honest in my marriage, or do I have certain secrets? Do I do things that displease, anger, or hurt my marriage-partner? What have I done to make him or her especially happy in some way?

If I am unmarried, do I accept it as God's will? Do I keep the proper distance from persons bound in marriage?

Am I clear in understanding that Christ condemned the remarriage of divorcees as adultery?

THE SEVENTH COMMANDMENT: Thou shalt not steal.

Have I evaded taxes due or misappropriated goods or monies entrusted to me? Have I taken part in what is really shady or illegal business?

Have I harmed anyone materially—the people or establishment for which I work, for example—by rendering bad or inadequate service for good pay?

Do I manage my own household or property justly? Or am I miserly, possessive, or wasteful?

Are my outlays and expenses in fact much smaller than they should be? Am I ready to make real sacrifices?

THE EIGHTH COMMANDMENT: Thou shalt not bear false witness against thy neighbor.

Have I been sincere in my speech and in all my behavior?

Have I fawned upon or "buttered up" anyone or attempted to make myself liked or needed by flattery?

Do I wish to appear better than I am?

Have I respected the honor of others, or have I spoken evil or untruth about a person? Have I transmitted or allowed gossip about others? Have I spoken, without necessary reason, of the bad side of any person?

Is there someone from whom I should beg pardon?

Have I spoken up in defense of victims of calumny? Have I kept secrets with which I have been entrusted?

THE NINTH AND TENTH COMMANDMENTS:
Thou shalt not covet thy neighbor's house. Or set thy heart upon thy neighbor's wife, or servant or handmaid or ox or ass or anything else that is his.

Am I content with what I have, or do I always want more? Am I ready to recognize the limits God has placed on my person or life?

Am I ready to accept everything that comes from the hand of God—whether wealth or poverty, health or illness, happiness or suffering?

Have I harmed a person's reputation? Have I undermined his life situation or happiness in any way?

Have I involved myself unjustly in the affairs of others? Have I sown unrest or trouble?

What is my *main weakness*? What have I been doing to overcome it?

AN EXAMINATION OF CONSCIENCE

I quite understand, God says, that one should examine one's
    conscience.
It is an excellent practice. It should not be abused.
It is even recommended. It is quite right.
Everything which is recommended is right.
And besides it is not only recommended. It is prescribed.
Consequently it is quite right.

But at last you are in bed. What do you mean by self-examination, examining your conscience?

If it means thinking of all the stupid things you have done during the day, if it means reminding yourself of all the stupid things you have done during the day,

With a feeling of repentance, though perhaps I should not say of contrition,

But anyway with a feeling of penitence which you offer me, all right, that's quite right,

I accept your penitence. You are decent people, good fellows.

But if it means sifting through and ruminating at night over all the thanklessness of the day,

All the fevers and all the bitterness of the day,

And if it means you want to chew over at night all the stale sins of the day,

Your stale fevers and your regrets and your repentances and your remorse which is staler still,

And if it means you want to keep an accurate register of your sins,

Of all those stupidities and of all those idiocies,

No, let me keep the Book of Judgment myself.

Perhaps you will be the gainer into the bargain.

*   *   *   *   *

. . . When the pilgrim, when the guest, when the traveller

Has trailed for hours through the muddy highways,

Before crossing the threshold of the church he carefully wipes his feet,

Before going in,

Because he is very tidy.

And the mud from the roads must not soil the flag-stones in
 the church.
But once it is done, once he has wiped his feet before
 entering,
Once he has gone in he no longer thinks of his feet,
He is not always looking to see if his feet are properly wiped.
He has no heart, he has no eyes, he has no voice any more
Except for the altar where the Body of Jesus
And the memory and the expectation of the Body of Jesus
Shine eternally.

—From *The Mystery of the Holy Innocents and Other Poems* by Charles Péguy, translated by Pansy Pakenham (New York, Harper & Row, 1957), pp. 80–81. Reprinted by permission of Harper & Row, Publishers.

Bibliography

The following is a selective list of works which, in the judgment of the author, can be of assistance in pursuing more deeply the various themes we have touched on in the course of this book.

GENERAL LITERATURE

The New Testament especially, but also the Old Testament, particularly the prophetic books.

Fries, Heinrich, ed., *Handbuch theologischer Grundbegriffe*, 2 vols. Munich, 1962–63.

Rahner, Karl, *Schriften zur Theologie*, 5 vols. Einsiedeln, Zurich, Cologne, 1954 ff., and various editions. Special reference is made to the sections on the sacrament of penance in vols. II and III.

———, *The Christian Commitment*. New York, Sheed and Ward, 1963.

———, *Theology for Renewal*. New York, Sheed and Ward, 1964.

———, *The Christian in the Marketplace*. New York, Sheed and Ward, 1966.

Rahner, Karl, and Vorgrimler, Herbert, *Theological Dictionary*. New York, Herder and Herder, 1965.

SPECIALIZED LITERATURE

Anciaux, Paul, *The Sacrament of Penance*. New York, Sheed and Ward, 1962.

Barton, John M. T., *Penance and Absolution*. New York, Hawthorn, 1961.

Böhme, W., *Beichtlehre für evangelische Christen*. Stuttgart, 1956.

Bommer, J., *Von der Beichte und vom Beichten*, 2d ed. Luzern-Munich, 1962.

Hopfenbeck, G., *Beichtseelsorge*, 2d ed. Werl. in W. 1960.

Kelin, L., *Evangelisch-lutherische Beichte. Lehre und Praxis*. Paderborn, 1961.

Lackmann, M., *Wie beichten wir?*, 2d ed. Gütersloh, 1950.

Monden, Louis, S.J., *Sin, Liberty and Law*, New York, Sheed and Ward, 1965.

Planck, O., *Evangelisches Beichtbüchlein*, 2d ed. Stuttgart, 1957.

Pohle, Joseph, *The Sacraments*, Vol. II, *Penance*. St. Louis, Herder, 1946.

Riga, P., *Sin and Penance*. Milwaukee, Bruce, 1962.

Rondet, H., *The Theology of Sin*. Notre Dame, Fides, 1960.

Saint-Séverin, Community of, *Confession: The Meaning and Practice of the Sacrament of Penance*. Westminster, Newman Press, 1959.

Sheerin, John B., *Sacrament of Freedom*. Milwaukee, Bruce, 1961.

Snoeck, André, *Confession and Pastoral Psychology*. Westminster, Newman Press, 1961.

——, *Confession and Psychoanalysis*. Westminster, Newman Press, 1964.

Thurian, Max, *Confession*. Naperville, Allenson, 1958.

Tilmann, K., *Die Führung zu Busse, Beichte, und christlichem Leben*. Würzburg, 1961.

Van Zeller, Dom Hubert, *Approach to Penance*. New York, Sheed and Ward, 1958.

Watkins, Oscar D., *A History of Penance*. New York, B. Franklin, 1960.

Wilson, Alfred, *Pardon and Peace*. New York, Sheed and Ward, 1947.